TAKE MY HAND TO THE PROMISED LAND

Sandy Hardy
Take My Hand To The Promised Land

Published by BooxAI

ISBN: 978-965-578-210-3

TAKE MY HAND TO THE PROMISED LAND

SANDY HARDY

CONTENTS

DEDICATION

Hand to hand we can take the land and love one another. As Christ wants us to love him unconditionally. Loving one another, dare you show your love and honor him?

This book is for you, to show you who our Father is, how wonderful and amazing he is, that we can do all things by him, who strengthens us. Don't waste time, years not knowing him, open your heart to him now, and know him as your personal savior.

A special shout out to our new generation preachers, as each week I look so forward to receiving the word.

Steven (Larry) Furtick and Pastor Holly Furtick, are a few of the new now generation pastors and are very good. My personal thoughts on they are driven and bring it.

You have such a tremendous number of fabulous ministers out there to choose from and to hear and receive the word of God. Start your journey today. You can go in person or stream and enjoy the gifts of all. An especially nice ministry also is Pastor Dharius Daniels and his wife, Pastor Shameka Daniels. Such an amazing selection to choose from to hear the word of GOD. Upcoming change is what we need to bring unity, and not diversion. To bring honor, love, and togetherness among one another.

Love for Christ.

Stand up for God.

My LORD, My King. You are amazing. My hero; I can never thank you enough for all you are. My dedication is to you Lord, to bring you Glory. In the context of being thankful, I want to reach out to my son Brad, and let him know I am very proud of him and love him very much. To my grandchildren Callen and Emeree, may the good Lord perfect your gifts and look down upon you. My daughter-in-law Jalea and my dear Sara.

To my dear friends and my sister's Lexis and Judy, I love you all very much. I pray the good Lord blesses you always. Craig Wooldridge whom I have known since five years old, has been an inspired me and encouraged me along this journey, and someone, who can always make you smile. Thank you.

To Jim, who loved the Lord beyond words and knew when to bring it. I love you with all my heart. You are in a special place right now and there is not a day, you are not missed. Thank you for all you are and everything you brought to me.

This is also dedicated to you. My love and hope that you may find Christ as your personal savior and know the love that passes all understanding.

Sandy

INTRODUCTION

The title of this book is called, Take My Hand to the Promised Land. Appropriately named with honoring our heavenly father. To take some things that another or others have gone through and try to help another to endure the pain, share what they individually suffered, and help to release the same, whereas, they do not have to have the same, provide a buffer, and to release yourself into the loving arms of the heavenly father and grow, develop a personal relationship with our father and son. Where he, God, says he will be there and never leave or forsake you, he will take your hand, he will open his arms, and you can cast, yes, cast all your cares upon him. We were not designed to carry all the world on our shoulders and neither are we created to be beaten, suffer, denied, or to live without our father and at the hands of another. We are his children and each one of us are called to do something special and each one of us, are very special.

We will go through many trials and tribulations, and they are not ours to choose or the timing of any of them either. How we present ourselves in them and during them is how we will come out/handle them and have an end result. With our father, we can, do anything. Surrender yourself unto him and come boldly to the throne. Ask and it shall be given. Know him. Love him. Honor him. Watch the manifestation of your life change as you present yourself humbly to him and walk in his ways. Dare to take the challenge, submit yourself to him, believe that Jesus died on the cross for your sins. Watch each day present itself into a wonderful life and journey that you were designed to take and how the good Lord will show you love, comfort and peace.

Time invested to know who your heavenly father is, is the best decision that, you will ever make. Happiness, joy, peace, love, prosperity is a few of the many things, that you can experience with the father and son. The decision you make today, you will never regret. The regret is not taking the time to know him. No matter how much comes against you, you will see that we have an amazing father in all things and in trying times. It is his purpose to know you and grow intimately with you. It is not what happens to you, it is what happens for you. Being always thankful in all things. I hope that you will see and come to know Christ and accept him as your personal savior. To be able to enjoy the most wonderful relationship that you may ever know or experience. That when you face something, you may go boldly to him and he will comfort you and answer you always. There is nothing in this world worth losing your joy or peace over and may your journey be a blessed one along with our heavenly father today and ever more!

TAKE MY HAND INTO THE PROMISED LAND

There are so many things that life brings and offers, yet where are you in this?

You have seen many things and evolved into things that you were broken into pieces about. You feel as if you have no place to turn.

Searching for answers and lost in the turmoil of it all.

No one to help and no one to turn to. You say who cares and what is the point. It is a place of despondency, and all do not understand you.

Why, why me??

The anger surges in, and the abandonment. You react to this event, no matter what it is and this is where it starts to be glorious for you.

He said, "Let there be light and there was." He is our mighty Father, "GOD."

You think this is not the answer or the way?

Dare to take this journey with me, and you will see, that he, God is the light.

CHAPTER 1

You think you have found the utmost love of your life; the actual start of the relationship was amazing in itself to say the least.

There was nothing in it, anyone could say, you were in love with them.

Every waking moment and in everyday, you made them the center of your attention.

No one could speak one word against them as you were at defense for them in all of it. No matter if it was your parent, a friend, and maybe even yourself.

Did you ever once go to God in prayer and ask him, where it fits? Did you ever once put God first, and put all down to run to him?

Did you ever refuse to listen to others encouraging your walk and relationship with God?

Then maybe, you can see, without the vision and the hand of God, maybe then the relationship was not meant to be in the first place.

Nothing without work... works.

Must believe that he, God our Father, exists and that he rewards those who seek him.

Scripture verses to read.

Luke 19: 10 For the son of man came to seek and save the lost.

Psalm 91: 11 ESV For he will command his angels concerning you to guard, to guard you in all your ways.

Hebrews 11: 6 ESV And without faith it is impossible to please him, for whoever would draw near to God must believe that he exists and that he rewards those who seek him.

Isaiah 41: 10 ESV Fear not, for I am with you. Be not dismayed, for I am your God, I will strengthen you, I will, keep you, I will uphold you with my righteous right hand.

CHAPTER 2

It is amazing to have the love of God. To be equally in love and awe of him. Just as amazing to be in a relationship of the flesh.

When you combine them both, the love in itself by itself is an aura of colors, feelings, and total connection and total giving of yourself. Complete surrender. That is like the explosion at a 4th of July festival. You can keep it alive, as when we surrender, God becomes our defender. A divine perfect love.

If you do not take the time to allow yourself the ability to love and to be loved, you are robbing yourself of the gift of love. We are to love one another as God so loved the world and all that is in it. A pure love and reflection of the perfection of who our father is. We can do nothing apart from our father. In itself, who would really desire to?

The intimate relationship that we have with the father is that unsurpassable by any relationship with one another, yet, joined together in his love, a love developed as his love for us. A Christian love. Wanting to please him and not man or woman, things, or other. His love flows through us, so we can reach out and share that love with each other. Grow, being fruitful and multiplying are the most amazing gifts he can give us. He gave his son, so that our sins could be forgiven, and that is the most total love ever imaginable. Each and every day is a true and divine blessing from him, and we should cherish it and everyone we have been given as a treasured gift from God above.

If for some reason, you are sitting back and going through things because of a broken relationship, and there is nothing more tragic than a broken relationship, it is by him that it says he will give you strength. God will supply all your needs. Be still, and rest in him. Not by power or might, but by my spirit, you will succeed. God is awesome... and so are you. Envision the journey and happiness that our father has for you and see where that leads you. No one ever said it was going to be an easy road, but you can, with one foot in front of the other, take steps to go forward. Even when you are knocked down or knocked back, hold on...because he has the greatest plans for you ahead. The loss of a loved one, be it through death, abuse, abandonment, or anything relatedly associated, remember, you and they were connected for a reason. The love and the connection were there, the love. Embrace it as a gift from God, and treasure it. It belongs to you. No person can tell you how long to grieve over anything. We are all unique in our process patterns. Sharing with, I lost the love of my life through desertion. Someone I spent twenty-plus years with. Drug me through court another plus seventeen years. I spent many years loving this person and thought I would not make it. The crying would not stop. I am not a crier. I finally got tired of it and went to see a physician, and he told me that we are all different and grieve. It is a process, and when we grieve, we are not hurting for one person or things, it is all that has encompassed us in losses throughout or lives that we did not deal with or recognize at the time of losing them it or other. Crying is good for you; it cleans out the impurities and toxins. That made sense to me, so much that shortly after, I stopped crying. I did not embrace the process of when my mother died and other events that happened. I stuffed them down, so I could be strong for others. Not to mention that it created panic attacks. The door is open for those who love him. Our heavenly father loves us, and his love is real. He will never desert you or abandon you. There are answers to questions that he may reveal to you, but there are also answers until you meet again, he will tell you then. It really is not for us to know, and we are to stand strong and be full of courage, knowing he is taking our hand and is in control of all. Thank the Lord, and the time you had. Even if it was unbelievably bad, love and forgive. Forgive them. You must forgive so that your heart can be receptive to love and to be loved. God knows everything and when his child, yes, we are all his children, whether we are babies are we are seniors, and hurting, he knows. You say they do not deserve to be forgiven, they did this and they did that. It is for you and your well-being to be able to forgive, and to move forward towards the divine purpose God, has in store for you. If you do not forgive, you become a walking poison. It eats and festers in you and the place where the Lord wants you to be. God knows everything and sees all, in his time, he will take care of things. We are never to wish ill will on anyone and this is a human emotion. He says, he will take care of our enemies. So, in that, take his hand and let him guide you to where he wants you to go. No one person in the world is worth ruining yourself or your life over. They are out doing what they want, not concerned in the least and having a wonderful time while you are agonizing over it. Wasting what could be the best day and time of your life. Work on building a relationship with God and look forward to what he has in store for you and the blessings. That is his destiny, he has designed it for you. Embrace it.

Embrace him. God is our provider and you can accomplish everything with and through him. It is futile to hold onto something that you have no control over! It is best to move forward and enjoy the journey. Sojourning does nothing but allow you to float and make excuses for not being obedient. It will amaze you to step back and watch how amazing our father is. You may have thought that this person was everything, however, if it was meant to be, you would most definitely be with them. No one said it would be easy, but you yourself will make it hard on you by yourself. While you are brooding over a break-up, they are out enjoying themselves and not concerned in the least. Sometimes people need a break and then rejoin or reconnect in the future. If it is a loss through death or other, it is most certainly a time to take and reflect on them and allow God, to comfort you, and he most certainly will in every way. A divorce even feels like a death, and it consists of their family, as it is a connection of unity that combines both families. It does not have to be; however, it is a strong person and two, you and them, that can make it work. Love is kind and patient. God is good. It is up to you to step back and step out and make time to develop your relationship with the Lord. In itself, it is by far the best journey and relationship you will ever have. In all things, honor him. He will see you through. Whatever you decide to do, do something that is good for you.

Every day is a gift. Every day God has blessings for you. Do not waste it by pouring over what could have been. The hurt overwhelms you, where, you do not press on and see the destiny that God has in store for you and what you are supposed, to be doing with your life. Enjoy everyone and everything you have been given. You are loved. Not just today, but always. God, will never desert you or abandon you. Being abandoned is not kind, yet forgives them. It is something that they have lost and must deal with. Turn it over to the Lord. You will love again and again.Embrace the memories you have

of them and hold them dear. That can't be taken away from you. However, do not make it a shrine where you go daily. Allow yourself time to be who you are and "Breathe." The ability you have, to love is the greatest gift God has given you. He gave his son to die for our sins, and that is the most supreme gift of all. Relationships will come and go and in it you, yourself grow. The best relationship is with God and it is eternal. With and in God, you can develop a lasting relationship with someone and flourish. God does not want you sad or beaten down and broken. Go along with God, strive to set out for the love and happiness that God destined for you and your future. No one has a right to rob, deny, or take anything from you. You have a gift and let it shine in his hands. Take the first step today and stand to declare you are his and you will succeed. Allow yourself the time of loss and grieve. Know that there is nothing you alone can do about it. Selling yourself short, not going in the direction God ordained you to go in is a waste of your time and your life. If God, wants this to be, then embrace it. Hug yourself totally and wipe the tears away, and let God direct your path and your steps. Get up and get moving. Now...

John: 3-16 KJV God so loved the world that he gave his one and only Son that whoever believes in him shall not perish.

Psalms 63: 1-7 KJV Oh, God, thou art my God early will I seek thee; my soul thirsteth for thee, my flesh longeth for thee in a dry and thirsty land, where no water is in it.

1-113. Because thy loving kindness is better than life, my lips shall praise thee.

7. Because thou hast been my help, therefore in the shadow of thy wings, I will rejoice.

Jeremiah 31: 3 KJV The Lord hath appeared of old unto me saying, Yes, I have loved thee with an everlasting love: therefore, with loving kindness, have I drawn thee.

Jeremiah 33: 3 KJV Call unto me, and I will answer thee, and show thee great and mighty things, which thou knowest not.

Deuteronomy 6:5 KJV And thou shall love the Lord thy God with all thine heart and with all thy soul, and with all thy might.

Romans 5:8 ESV But God shows his love for us in that while we were still sinners, Christ died for us.

John 14: 6 ESV Jesus said to him "I am the way, and the truth, and the life. No one comes to the father except through me."

John 15:5 ESV I am the vine; you are the branches, whoever abides in me

and I in him, he it is that bears much fruit, for apart from me you can do nothing.

James 4 6:10 ESV But he gives more grace. Therefore, it says, "God opposes the proud., but gives grace to the humble. "Submit yourselves therefore to God, resist the devil, and he will flee from you. Draw near to God, and he will draw near to you. Cleanse your hands, you sinners and purify your hearts, you double minded. Be wretched and mourn and weep. Let your laughter be turned to mourning and your joy turned to gloom. Humble yourselves before the Lord, and he will exalt you.

1 Timothy 6: 12-16 ESV Fight the good fight of the faith. Take hold of the eternal life to which you were called and about which you made the good confessions in the presence of many witnesses. I charge you in the presence of God, who gives life to all things, and of Christ Jesus, who in his testimony before Pontius Pilate made the good confession, to keep the commandment unstained and free from reproach until the appearing of our Lord Jesus Christ, which he will display at the proper time- he who is the blessed and only Sovereign, the King of kings and Lord of lords, who alone has immortality, who dwells in unapproachable light whom no one has ever see or can see. To him be honor and total dominion. Amen.

Galatians 2:20 ESV I have been crucified with Christ, it is no longer I who live, but Christ who lives in me. And the life I now live in the flesh I live by faith in the Son of God, who loved me and gave himself for me.

CHAPTER 3

You have worked extremely hard for the position that you are in and there is a promotion, or you are extremely overworked, to the point of burn- out. Do you give up? Do you just endure? No, you place it into God's hands and allow him to move you and the situation and see where he guides you. My peace, I give unto you. If there is time allowed, you may even take off and allow it to be an enjoyable time while God is in control and while resting in his care, conditions can become very favorable for you. He may even have a change in things that you have always wanted to do, and you are given a chance to finally do. Such as a new venture, a new hobby, starting your own business, whatever it is, dare to take the chance that God has given you for your designed destiny. You may be missing out because you will not allow God, to flow through you. You may be well surprised. It does not seem right that you must endure something that you are not meant to do, and that is not governing his will for your life. It sure is not happiness to just be getting through. If you can envision it, you can achieve it. God says, faith as small as a mustard seed can move moun- tains. Do you not have faith more than a seed?? Everything is there for you. I would not say to try and do them all at once, however, you can see something set your sight on the goal and go for it. There are no fail- ures, just failing in trying. You are a child of the highest and he will be with you along the way and always. If it is not your destiny, your spirit guide will tell you. God is with you forever. God has the best in store for you, and it is up to you to allow God to flow through you. You are the best and you can do anything you set your mind to doing. Dare give yourself a chance and do it. There is not I can't. Small efforts grow and turn into success. Father and son are there for you. Jesus came so we could have life more abundantly. He died the ultimate price for our sins. Certainly, you can give yourself a chance and honor him. He is well pleased with you. Take the limits off of yourself, as it is not you, it is that you are letting emotions and feelings rule you, and that my dear is not an option. When you are feeling like that, go to the word and let God speak to you. Be quiet and allow that time with him to saturate into your core and follow him. The rest and peace God so graciously gifts to you are unexplainable. A feeling that you would like to bottle and open. By building a relationship with our father you can have that peace and joy always.

Certainly, he does not want to see you hurting, or are down. There is not any human being alive worth losing days over, time over, ruining your life over, or even contemplating taking your life and giving up. You miss out on the wonderful things God has ordained for your life and your purpose is on hold by those. The person, no matter who they are, are not thinking about you. They are not looking back, and they are probably more than likely enjoying themselves and moving on to what their destiny has for them. Do not allow anything to rob you of your joy and who you are. I can promise you it is not worth it. God is everything. Give yourself a chance. I can't impress that not to allow the circumstances to alter, defer, or take from you.

You are equipped to do all he has set out for you to do. It does not matter what it is. We all have a special gift and talent God has given us to do, and we should honor and reverence him and do our best at everything. Nothing comes easy, but with perseverance, you shall achieve to do and be all he has destined for you to do. Be happy. Share that happiness and maybe focus on someone else rather than yourself. In time anything that frustrates, can be changed by taking on a different mindset and doing something constructive. Music, walking, laughing, reading a book, dancing, any outlet that gives you freedom from feeling down, pick-up and do. Dedicate something onto yourself to make you happy. Before long, you will see changes and the joy it promotes. God gives peace and joy. By prayer and supplication, go to him. Even if you have another goal and are in a position where is just mundane, being tolerated, work and pray towards the goals, you would like to do and see happen. He gives you grace for each new day.

2 Corinthians 12:9 NIV But he said to me, "My grace is sufficient for you, for my power is made perfect in weakness." Therefore, I will boast even more gladly about my weaknesses."

Jeremiah 29:11 NIV For I know the plans I have for you, declares the Lord, plans to prosper you and not to harm you, plans to give you hope and a future.

Zechariah 4:6 KJV For he answered and spake to unto me, saying, this is the word of the Lord unto Zerubbabel saying, Not by might, nor by power, but, by my spirit, saith the Lord of hosts.

Philippians 4:6 ESV Do not be anxious about anything but in everything by prayer and supplication with thanksgiving let your requests be known to God.

CHAPTER 4

If you are new to the word, pick it up and start reading. Join a church, listen on television, and give yourself forty days, as the people in the wilderness walking around, as Jesus did and you will start to see a different person altogether. You will be yearning for Christ and the beautiful journey and life he has in store for you. Transformation begins with you. The relationship begins with you. Knock, and he will answer, as he has already been there by your side waiting on you. Arms opened.

Sharing mine with you, I have been there for others and tried to meet their needs the best way I can. When all is said and done, satisfied, they are not ever really satisfied. They turn on you and abandon you. No reason or explanation. Reaching out because it hurts, you try and give more of yourself. Being the better person and taking on an entirely new course. Not retaliating or anger. It is hard. No one ever said things would be easy. We are to be content in all things and through all things. I was so discouraged and down, I pray for them and keep praying our father will make a way through this. Not understanding why. It has been some time and as it is written, it is in his perfect timing, not ours. We want our way. We want to control things. We can't do it. We can't do anything alone but, we, father, son and holy spirit, can take on the world and together, we CAN, do this together. I was sitting and having my pity party and getting down about it as I said, it hurts. It hurts greatly. Then it came and was said, people abandon me and do not know me, yet I am here with my arms opened.

Loving them and welcoming them. It is the same. I do not turn my back on them but am open to them coming to me. I realized then that Jesus has been crushed and hurt deeply, yet he has a loving and huge heart. Who am I to want to have this fixed? I can love and continue to love as our father has so done to all of us. Having hope and faith that, in his timing, this will heal and reconnect with my loved one. Patience. He is so awesome and if the time daily is given to be obedient unto him, you will have blessings unimaginable and a relationship you want to sing about. Happiness is the walk with him. Everyone is always looking to be happy and find the key to happiness. The key to happiness is simply the decision to be happy and make it so. Join yourself with a wonderful union with God. There is no greater gift. There also is no other happiness you will experience quite like the relationship you have with God. Added to that onto your life is an exceptional exhilaration of true joy.

In this, I also was shown that one mentioned as to being hurt by is my own child. Not brought up this way. In marriage, it was by his partner's choice and that he, has acted. Not in God's way, but we make choices sometimes that are not in line with our heavenly fathers. You have to have love for God in order to be able to love, and love for yourself also. They say a child is a gift by God. It is a very precious gift. In this, I heard a small voice saying is a gift for a brief time. Raise them up in the way which they should go. It is a gift that is so precious, as stated again, that the time you have with them is important. God has a life chosen for them and a journey to take. Just as Jesus had a journey and a purpose to fulfill. We as parents, are to love them unconditionally and support them no matter what. God said to Jesus, I am well pleased with you, my son. That is what we need to tell our children no matter what. The gift is God chose you to be their parent and you are to love them and parent them. God is there to be with them always, love them, guide them, and have the best relationship with them forever.

Sometimes, we have to let go, for them to have the life they were intended to lead. It is not about what hurt us, when younger or what someone did. Or even what you did not have. It is about realizing that you want the absolute best for them. God wants you to be encouraging and loving as he is. So, in this, I have to take a step back to let him, my son know, that I am proud of him and support him. Even in his actions towards me. At some point and time, he will get it, or we, will meet again. My love for him is real, and so is our heavenly father's love. Casting all your cares upon him. There is no simplified versions or easy answers. Trust is a big step. The pride you feel is the letter I. I this and I that. Stop putting the I in everything and reverse it into belief. Be, being, still... Divert the mindset on you to him. Otherwise, you will be frantic and suffer anxiety, and again both words have I in them. A known pastor on television has a particularly good sermon on this. Take the time to search, read, and listen. Most of all, allow yourself to grow. Do not let the devil, evil, take, or rob you of anything and most of all do not do this to yourself. You are your captain and God allows you to be so. He will be your captain and navigator and guide you on a fantastic journey. If you allow him to. You must be willing and to have an open heart. Accept him as your savior and watch the ebbs turn and the sea flow. He will excite you, and most of all he will be with you always. His arms are always open at any time and, waiting for you.

Proverbs 22:6 NIV Start children on the way they should go, and even when they are old, they will not turn from it.

Psalms 103 11-12 ESV For as high as the heavens are above the earth, so great is his steadfast love toward those who fear him; as far as the east is from the west so far does he remove our transgressions from us.

Peter 2 1 & 9 AMPC Beloved, I am now writing you this second letter, in (both of) them. I have stirred up your unsullied (sincere) mind by the way of remembrance.

9- The Lord does not delay and is not tardy or slow about what he promises, according to some people's conception of slowness, but he is long suffering (extraordinarily patient) toward you, not desiring that any should perish, but that all should turn to repentance.

1 John 4 8-12 NIV Whoever does not love does not know God, because God is love.

9 This is how God showed his love among us, He sent his one and only Son into the world that we might live through him.

10 This is love not that we loved God, but that he loved us and sent his Son an atoning sacrifice for our sins.

11 Dear friends, since God so loved us, we also ought to love one another.

12 No one has ever seen God, but if we love one another, God lives in us and his love is made complete in us.

1 Peter 5 7 KJV Casting all your care upon him, for he careth for you.

Revelation 3 20 KJV Behold, I stand at the door and knock; if any man hears my voice, and open the door, I will sup with him, and he with me.

CHAPTER 5

Don't let anyone hold you back. The world is an oyster and it is all created by our heavenly father. Don't let anything or anyone take from you what is rightfully yours. The beauty in all that God has created is, he created it for you. He created you and you are his most perfect creation. Appreciate all that is out there and embrace it all. Don't again, let anyone distract you, including yourself. There are no limits on anything you can do or be, only the limits you place upon yourself. With God and in God, you can do anything and conquer anything. Each day and moment are a step taken with him and in him, there is Victory. There is no greater love than the love God has to offer. He has no price on his love or conditions attached. The control you allow someone to have is the control you are placing on yourself and there are no excuses for that. Take his hand and you will see the beauty he has created and surrounds you. The other thing that was shown, is that in missing out on something and feeling sad about it, that in loss, there is a rainbow of joy that appears out of it, if you are willing to take the time to open your eyes and apply your senses to each one. First, the gift of, whether it be a relationship, a child, or even an unborn child, a disease, you have been given something by the father and it is not to let it over take you or overwhelm you. It may not even have an answer right away, but draw closer to him and he is known as our comforter.

The best yet is to come because if you take I can't from it, you will see, that you have a lot to give, you have the love that can be poured out to another that needs the love and your love. Just someone that wants a hug and you are able to give it, you will never know how much that means to another, or you need a hug. I am not usually someone that walks up to a stranger, but this infant had a picture, known as a Hallmark picture moment, waiting on his dad in a shopping cart, and had the worse smirk on his face you would ever want to see, to the point it was funny. As I was coming down the aisle, I gently touched his arm and told him to smile... as it was not particularly bad. My companion was alarmed because his father was nearby, and it startled him I touched this child. I laughed and his father said, he will smile when he wakes up. Yet, the time you take so simple can make it so different. I am not saying to go touch someone's child, but sometimes the moment calls for it and you can seize it. Or open a bag for an elderly person who can no longer do it and struggles in produce. Kindness goes a long way. God says take care of my flock. We are all his flock. It does not matter if someone does nothing for you or you are saying but, what about me, as it is not about you. It is about what is inside of you and doing it as a love for God.

Unto him, you yield. There is not any greater gift than the feeling you get inside that onto God, and acting as he does feels like inside. It is like a hot cup of chocolate sitting in front of a warm fire. He is so awesome and amazing.

Matthew 19-26 NIV Jesus looked at them and said, "With man, this is impossible, but with God all things are possible."

Psalm 139-14 ESV I praise you, for I am fearfully and wonderfully made. Wonderful are your works; my soul knows it very well.

Colossians 3-23 NIV Whatever you do, work at it with all your heart, as working for the Lord, not for human masters.

2 Timothy 1-7 NKIV For God has not given us a spirit of fear, but of power and of love and of a sound mind.

John 3-16 NIV For God so loved the world that he gave his one and only Son, that whoever believed in him shall not perish but have eternal life.

John 14 15-17 ESV If you love me, you will keep my commandments and I will ask the Father, and he will give you another Helper, to be with you forever, even the Spirit of truth, whom the world cannot receive, because it neither sees him nor knows him. You know him, for he dwells with you and will be in you.

Romans 8 15-16 NLT So you have not received a spirit that makes you fearful slaves. Instead, you received God's Spirit when he adopted you as his own children. "Now we call him, Abba, Father. For his Spirit joins with our spirit to affirm that we are God's children.

Ephesians 3-20 NKJV Now to Him that is able to do exceedingly abundantly above all that we are ask or think, according to the power that works in us.

1 Chronicles 16-25 NIV For great is the Lord and most worthy of praise he is to be feared above all gods.

1 Chronicles 29-11 NIV Yours, Lord, is the greatness and the power and the glory and the majesty and the splendor for everything in heaven and earth is yours. Yours, Lord is the kingdom; you are exalted as head over all.

CHAPTER 6

Wat am I feeling? I feel rushed and hot and cold and my mind racing. All of a sudden it feels like I am out of control and going to have a heart attack. Not to make light of this, as it could very well be a heart attack. Go see a doctor for care if you suspect this. However, it very well may be a panic attack. A disorder. What is it? Lots of people do not know, but it is able to be handled and taken care of. You may need medicine to aid the attacks, and you may be able to work through them yourself. However, the most effective way to deal with them, is with our heavenly father. It states and the father says, by his stripes, we are healed. We all must have something that weighs us down or something that the good Lord wants our attention over. If you read the Psalms, you will receive a lot of comfort in going through these. Asking me, what do I know about them? I went through them. Operative word, you are going through them and they do not control you. You control them. Yes, darling, you do have control over them. Even in the midst of a terrific one, you can deal with it. Stop. Take hold of, and quiet yourself, talk, count, think of something else, walk, whatever is your pleasure, and they will subside.

To me it is that you have so much upon you and overwhelmed, that it takes place considered to be a file box. When it gets full and you think you have everything in the world to do, it comes on you. Or you are doing something that you are fearful of, or that you feel guilty about. Whatever triggers it, you will soon become aware of. God says he has a perfect plan for you. You can let it control you and succumb to it, where it is crushing to the fact you are house bound and do not go out. It may take a while, but once you know what it is, you can handle it. God will see you through everything. Do not let it take hold of you because it is not going to do anything more than hinder you and create problems you do not need. It is treatable, and it is where you are strong in the lord and can do all things. You can also make it larger than it really is and give way to it. How you respond to it and all things is the outcome. Does it go away, I think in time yes, as you are the driver, and where you go within your thoughts and actions are the road as to where your destination will be. Certainly, it is alarming, but so is falling off a horse. You can do this. In all things, he will give you the rest and strength. Not by power or might but by his strength, you will succeed. He is so amazing.

Don't try and control yourself the feelings, and emotions are hundreds of daily, and to act on them, all causes great distress. If there is something that is important, then deal with it. However, you are not able to do God's job. He created the universe, you didn't. Let yourself feel his love. Take yourself out of the equation. There is nothing so important that it cannot wait, or that you have to put yourself and your wellbeing on the line for. God will direct your steps.

Allow him to work and be who he is, and you to be as you are and were created to be. Things do not happen in an instant. In all things, acknowledge him. Putting all that is concerning you into his hands. In today's world we are concerned about images, ego, thoughts, and not placing ourselves into his hands. There is so much there for you to do and be, you need to give yourself a chance. Images change as growth and age come for all. Do not ever let what anyone says or does become your all.

Most of the time, they are speaking about themselves if you will listen and connect the phrases stated. It is fine if someone is truly speaking constructively to you to better you. Don't take it internally and let it be your every waken moment reflecting on the words. They are words. That excites a reaction which triggers panic attack/attacks. We are all uniquely made.

Our father has made us in the likeness of him, and he does not go hither and from raging on end and having attacks. He is our creator and has overcome the world. You can overcome these attacks. Don't magnify them and you will see that they will go. If you do have them, will be far and few between and you can manage them. You can do all things by him. Don't allow this to cripple you. As you get closer to the door that the good Lord has for you, you will find more opposition, and the key to opposition is to stand and know who your father is. When tested, you pass the test. It may take a while and none of us can calculate the timing, but our father will never hurt you or leave you on your own. He is there and may even be carrying you when you are pushed where you think, your limits are and they are not. It is having the right mind set in the situation and events you are experiencing. Just as television has a remote control and you can change the channel or tune in. Change the channel and you will see the changes you so want to manifest for the better. In all things, stay in prayer over it. Even someone scaring you by going boo... could be called a panic attack because we would jump and be startled. This is a simple explanation of how it would feel. Let your father be your light and salvation. There is nothing too difficult for our heavenly father. Do not allow this to control you. You can overcome everything. There is a saying, our response to any given situation is that 10% is the actual action of the problem and 90% on how we respond. It is far better than to blow up, to stop, take a breath and do not give heed into it. In your journey and destiny, there is nothing in this world to become so engrossed in that it takes all from you. Life is short and should be enjoyed. Peace starts with you. Our brothers and sisters can become united if we start to make a difference and share love and peace. Passing it along. Even if, you are right, it does not really matter. You are not going to receive a Nobel peace prize. You are not going to be on Times Magazine, but what you will be, is obedient to Christ and living and doing as the Lord wants us to do. Change starts with you. Once you access the target of attacks, you will be successful in overcoming them. The Lord, says, not by power, or might, but by my spirit you will succeed. That stands by itself. Remember the Lord, created the universe and all that is in it. It all belongs to him. You are a child of the highest. He loves you. Open your arms to embrace him and receive his love. His peace passes all understanding, and you CAN DO THIS. It starts, with you. If your journey is designed to be on a magazine or to win the Nobel Peace prize, become a company owner, it is your destiny and nothing, can stop this. It is his will and his calling. We are to be the best at everything we do, working onto him, acknowledging him, and praising him.

Isaiah 43 18-19 KJV Remember ye not the former things, neither consider the things of old." Behold, I will do a new thing, now it shall spring forth; shall ye not know it? I will even make a way in the wilderness and rivers in the desert."

Colossians 3 1-4 NKJV If you were raised with Christ, seek those things which are above, where Christ is, sitting at the right hand of God. 2- Set your mind on things above, not on things on the earth. 3- For you died, and your life is hidden with Christ in God. 4- When Christ, who is our life appears, then you will also appear with him in glory.

Jeremiah 17 14 NIV Heal me, Lord, and I will be healed." Save me and I will be saved; for you are the one I praise.

Psalm 55-22 ESV Cast your burden on the Lord, and he will sustain you; he will never permit the righteous to be moved.

Mark 12 30 NIV Love the Lord your God with all your heart and with all your soul and with all your mind and with all your strength.

Proverbs 3 5-6 KJV Trust in the Lord with all thine heart; and lean not unto thine own understanding. In all thy ways, acknowledge him and he shall direct thy path.

Proverbs 16-9 ESV The heart of man plans his way, but the Lord establishes his steps.

Isaiah 48-17 ESV This says the Lord your redeemer, the Holy One of Israel "I am the Lord your God, who teaches you to profit; who leads you in the way you should go.

Isaiah 58-11 ESV And the Lord will guide you continually and satisfy your desire in scorched places and make your bones strong, and you shall be like a watered garden, like a spring of water, whose waters do not fail.

Psalm 37-3 KJV Trust in the Lord, and do good; so shalt thou dwell in the land and verily thou shalt be fed.

ISAIAH 12-2 NIV Surely God is my salvation; I will trust and not be afraid, the Lord, the Lord himself, is my strength and my defense.

Psalm 9-10 ESV And those who know your name put their trust in you, for you O Lord have not forsaken those who seek you.

Matthew 7-1 ESV & NKJV Judge not; that you not be judged. For with what judgment you judge, you will be judged; and with the measure you use, it will be measured back to you.

CHAPTER 7

If someone is out there calling you names and downgrading you, where you are hurting, you need to look in the mirror and see what is looking back at you. It is the most beautiful precious gift that God has created, and hey, it is YOU! Yes, you. Grasp that and see, God did not make any junk. He made us all differently and with special gifts and talents. Do you know what your talent is and what you enjoy? They say, you can never really call work, work, if you love doing what you are doing. That weekly piano training and football practices you go to, are forms to manifest a transformation as to what your destiny is, and no maybe you will not be the next tour on the road, or MBP, but that along with the journey will create the best God has in store for you, and the willingness, to see, if you are going to be that person that is on television and touring on the road. Don't block what gift God has given you. <u>You are the gift.</u> Bullying does not belong with you. Stand against it. Chances are the person who is the loudest is the weakest, and you can overcome it. God says, no weapon formed against you will prosper, and you have this right, not to allow anyone or anything to rob you of your joy. Even if they are ranting, chances are if you ignore them, and or even agree with them and laugh it off, it may develop into a lasting relationship or friendship. There are many reasons why others are mean. It may simply be because they do not have anything and you do and they are jealous. They could want the attention you get and they don't. Whatever it is, it is not up to you to determine the reason. You need to be the answer. Sometimes no matter how hard we try, it is never good enough, and then it is time to say the season has ended and be done with that. Not saying you can't be there for them; however, we can't fix people. You can be a friend and a friend indeed. No one has the right to push you, hit you or belittle you. If alone, you can make the decision not to be bullied and say nothing to keep the fight or their unkind actions to continue. One can't fight by themselves. It takes two to start a fight and one to be big enough to win by not giving into their actions. God does not allow his children to be hurt. If you are around a group, then it is best to try and quietly move away, call for help, do whatever it is to draw attention to you, that you may be in danger. Neighbor, teacher, police officer, phone emergency contact, whatever it is to protect and help another. We can also be united in standing with a friend or friends in not being part of a group to bully a person. God directs our steps and we even if in a group or with friends, and see this going on, can make a difference, by taking a stand. Be strong and of good courage. Right is right and wrong is wrong. No person ever has any right or a right to hurt another person. Be it by bullying, hitting, or emotionally attacking. Don't put yourself in a dangerous position ever. The things people say you have control over, not to let them upset you or to infect you. Yes, infect. Once it is said, tell yourself you are God's child and you belong to him. Nothing can come to harm you with his protection. Most of the time, hurting people hurt others. Infecting yourself with nothing is a waste of time, and it tears you down, with what you allow to come in. Swipe to the right and keep it moving. Smiles are contagious. Might even take off guard by agreeing with them and thanking them. Shocking to say the least, they do not expect that response. It is to hard each day, to let someone say something that really does not matter. Sometimes even if we, are right, the other person wants to disagree and argue, it is nicer to handle it, telling them, they are right. The air lifts and nothing is that important, that you want to be the warrior and have a knock down drag out fight over. What is the outcome of that?

Nothing. Put your time into something else. Getting even is not imbedded in you or part of your core. Vengeance belongs to the Lord, pray for this person or these parties. Just because someone else is different from you does not mean that person does not have feelings. You can open your arms to include them in your events and maybe see that they are a welcome part of you or a group. Most of the time, the people you are around now, while in school or other does not last a life time, however, a friendship formed can last a life time. You are not better than anyone else and no one is better than you are. We are all children of the lord. He did not separate his flock, and when one went missing, he, would separate to go and find the one missing. Seek his ways and be obedient to him. We are all different in one form or another, and be it that we, were all the same in everything it would be boring and become boring extremely fast. So sometimes, we lift each other by the talents that we have. We should also learn to appreciate the talents that someone else has and enjoy them for that. You have yours to share and they have theirs to share, and together it can be a very enjoyable time. Iron sharpens iron. You also must remember that not only do people bully in school but all levels of society. A boyfriend or a girlfriend can not only bully but emotionally try and manipulate you as well and bring you down but we will discuss this in another chapter. The best thing to do is to remember whose you are and you are a child of the highest God, our heavenly father. Thou it may hurt and you want to fight back, he has created you to soar beyond that. In remembering how Jesus was treated, and he paid the utmost price to die for our sins, you most certainly can ignore the insults and rebuke the person who is casting out hurtful actions, words and plain being mean.

Invoke peace. Be the solution. Be strong, courageous, and firm, fear not nor be in terror before them, for it is the Lord your God, who goes with you. He will, make a way before you. The person that is bullying you or belittling you, is not someone you want to engage with. It is like if there was someone at your door, ringing it, with a beautiful present. You open the door and they have the present, who does it belong to? It belongs to them. Let them keep it, do not pick it up, close the door, and they own the present of remorse and they carry it with them. Allowing the heavenly father to flow with and directly through you. The evil allows derision and it is in your life everywhere you go, and it is up to you to ignore and allow the word of God to penetrate your path, your direction and love. We are to show the light and how our father would act, if it were him in the same situation.

1 Peter 3-15 ESV But in your hearts honor Christ the Lord as holy, always being prepared to make a defense to anyone who asks., you for a reason for the hope that is in you; yet do it with gentleness and respect.

Proverbs 22-29 ESV Do you see a man skillful in his work? He will stand before kings; he will not stand before obscure men.

2 Peter 1-21 ESV For no prophecy was ever produced by the will of man, but men spoke from God as they were carried along by the Holy Spirit.

James 4 11-12 KJV Speak not evil one of another, brethren. He that speaketh evil of his brother, and judgeth his brother speaketh evil of the law; and judgeth the law; but if thou judge the law, thou art not a doer of the law but a judge.

4-31 KJV Ephesians Let all bitterness, and wrath, and anger, and clamor, and evil speaking, be put away from you with all malice.

Proverbs 17-9 KJV He that covereth a transgression seeketh love; but he that repeateth a matter separateth very friends.

Luke 37-38 ESV Judge not, and you will not be judged, condemn not, and you will not be condemned, forgive and you will be forgiven, give and it will be given to you.

Proverbs 15-1 NIV A gentle answer turns away wrath, but a harsh word stirs up anger.

Isaiah 54-17 NKJV No weapon formed against you shall prosper, and every tongue which rises against you in judgment you shall condemn. This is the heritage of the servants of the Lord and their righteousness is of me saith the Lord.

Joel 3-10 NKJV Beat your plowshares into swords. And your pruning hooks into spears; "Let the weak say, I am strong."

Psalm 91-4 ESV He will cover you with his pinions, And under his wings you will find refuge "His faithfulness is a shield and a buckler."

Ecclesiastes 3-1 ESV For everything there is a season, and a time for every matter under heaven.

Psalm 104-19 ESV He made the moon to mark the seasons; the sun knows it's time for setting.

Galatians 6-9 ESV And let us not grow weary of doing good, for in due season we will reap, if we do not give up.

CHAPTER 8

There are things that you have and others have not. It all belongs to God, as he created the world and all that is in it. Some of us are gifted in that our parents are able to provide those things by their jobs and levels of position, where some are working to make their families work and have the things they can provide. Key word is their parents and they are working. It is a difference in the salary that they have. It is no difference than the love they all have. Just because one friend has this and that, and you do not, does not make them different. One thing we do have and that is GOD's Love.

Material things are not important and will not last a life time. They also do not make you any different either. Whether you drive a Mercedes Bentz or a VW, you wear Gucci, or you shop other, you are the person inside these God created. Be thankful for all that you have and are given. God knows our needs and we individually need to come before him and make our requests known. There is also something called getting a job and working towards your goals and desires. He supplies all and through prayer and supplication, God, will supply your needs accordingly to his riches. You are saying, I am only 10 or 13, well you can have car washes, cupcake sales, walk someone's dog, whatever you can do to earn what it is, that you are wanting, and I can tell you, the events in doing this, and when you have enough to buy it finally, you will enjoy and appreciate it more, or maybe, you see, that in hard work, you may not even want it at this time. You can be a servant to him and donate it to someone else that is in need also, and this is so rewarding in itself that blessings, chase you down. If you are of an age where you can get a job, sometimes even having two jobs, will get you to where you can make that purchase. Only, do not cut yourself short out of an education for material things. Education is important and you should always have two choices as to what you want to do and achieve in your education. It is your book that the good lord has designed for you before you were even born. You can't fill your parent's shoes. That is their journey, and of course, you very well may follow as an attorney, doctor, banker, store owner, or whatever, but ultimately, it is what you desire and brings you happiness, that counts. What God preordained for you to do. One thing for sure, what you bring to it, put your best into it. In all things he will comfort you and bring you rest and peace. Parent's may not like this, but the truth is we are, set apart from people, which includes our parents. We want what is best for them, but, we cannot live their lives for them, or choose their lives for them. Go boldly to the throne and pray for God to direct you and your steps. Just arguing with them over and over is not productive for anyone. It is just pride that is hurt and hurting. Be grateful for them. We are loved by our father and he is amazing. Just as you are an amazing son/daughter. You are amazing mothers and fathers. You are a family. With and in God, you are his family, which he adores and loves you very much. Jesus went out into the world and preached the gospel. His parents went looking for him when he was out with the priests and the world teaching the word of God, so they did not choose his path of direction. Embrace what the Lord has in store for you and enjoy the incredible journey. God did not want you to live a just get by life. If you are a wife and mother, husband and father, be the best. If you are a teacher, janitor, attorney, be your best. We are not working to please people; we are to please and be pleasing to God. There are seasons for everything, and he most definitely will lead you to where you are supposed to go. You need to be willing and open unto him. Timing is his to decide, and it can take a second to many, many years and at the right moment and his moment, you will see his divine light shine down upon you. Wait patiently upon and on him. God's promises are forever and he never breaks a promise. When it says to turn it over to him and pray about it, it means to turn it over completely to God. Letting go and placing it into his hands. When you try and pick it up, you are placing doubt there and trying to control it yourself.

That is saying you turn it over to him but you do not believe unless you enter that it will be. It is total surrender and placing it totally into his hands and knowing he, will answer you. Of course, if it is not within his ways, it won't be answered as to cause someone harm, hurt someone or other that is not into conformity of our Lord. To also say, have you turned your life over to God, and believe that Jesus died for your sins? It is so amazing the relationship and life you can have walking hand and hand in and with the Lord. The joy, happiness and peace are an entirely new way of life to live and walk in. Shedding off the old way and ways. Looking forward to a joy filled day every day, and a peace, that passes all understanding. His peace. In your 40-day journey, you should be experiencing this loving relationship. He is. He is always happy to embrace you and cover and shower you with his love. Whatever it is, you should be able to go to him with everything. Wait upon him and let your light shine.The things that you want, pray and pray to him about them. He wants to abundantly bless you. All belong to him and if it is his desire for you to have them, he will bless you with them. Having a car to get to work, to school, to shop is a blessing, and it does not have to be a top-of-the-line car, name brand. It may even be a gift to another when buying another car, instead of trading it in, that you pass it onto another who has a need. Often than not, you will not get a trade in value when purchasing a new vehicle, but more than what could be counted as a trade in towards your next purchase is donating it to someone that really needs it. To take their children to school, to the doctor, to go to work, to take care of an ailing parent. That is the best trade there is, and God see's all and knows all.

The joy in your heart at giving is indescribable and is so welcomed in another's plight. It is also not about receiving and wanting all the time, it is about having a giving heart. Don't be dismayed at if you are praying about something and it is not forth-coming, as our father wants us to have, but in his timing, and it maybe that he wants you to have more, or a direction at to where he wants you to go and what he wants you to do. His will be done. Always trusting in him. Leaning is not in your own understanding. There is a season for everything. Lastly, you are not known by your possessions. God knows you as his daughter, his son, and his child. Be pleasing to him.

1 Timothy 6 9-10 NIV Those who want to get rich fall into temptation and a trap and into many foolish and harmful desires that plunge people into ruin and destruction. 10 For the love of money is the root of all kinds of evil. Some people, eager for money, have wandered from the faith and pierced themselves with many griefs.

James 4 2-4 NIV You desire but do not have, so you kill. You covet but you cannot get what you want, so you fight. You do not have because you do not ask God. When you ask, you do not receive, because you ask with wrong motives, that you may spend what you get on your pleasures. You adulterous people, don't you know that friendship means enmity against God? Therefore, anyone who chooses to be a friend of the world becomes an enemy of God.

Luke 12 15 NIV Then he said to them, watch out. Be on your guard against all kinds of greed; life does not consist in an abundance of possessions.

1 John 2 16-17 ESV For all that is in the world the desires of the flesh and the desires of the eyes and pride of life- is not from the Father but it is from the world. And the world is passing away along with its desires, but whoever does the will of God abides forever.

Matthew 10 38-39 NIV Whoever does not take up their cross and follow me is not worthy of me. Whoever finds their life will lose it, and whoever loses their life for my sake will find it.

Matthew 22 37-40 NIV James replied" Love the Lord your God with all your heart and with all your mind. This is the first and greatest commandment. And the second is like it; Love your neighbor as your-self. All the Love and the Prophets hang on these two commandments.

Proverbs 3 9-10 NIV Honor the Lord with your wealth, with the first fruits of all your crops; then your barns will be filled to over flow-ing, and your vats will brim over with new wine.

Ephesians 1 22-23 NIV And God placed all things under his feet and appointed him to head over everything for the church, which is his body, the fullness of him who fills everything in every way.

Colossians 3-17 ESV And whatever you do in word or deed, do everything in the name of the Lord Jesus, giving thanks to God the Father through him.

Exodus 20-3 ESV You shall have no other gods before me.

Luke 16 15 ESV And he said to them, "You are those who justify yourselves before men, but God knows your hearts. For what is exalted among men is an abomination in the sight of God".

1 Chronicles 28 9 ESV And you, Solomon my son, know the God of your father and serve him with a whole heart and with a willing mind, for the Lord searches all hearts and understands every plan and thought. If you seek him, he will be found by you, but if you forsake him, he will cast you off forever.

Proverbs 31 30 ESV Charm is deceitful, and beauty is vain, but a woman who fears the Lord is to be praised.

John 7 24 ESV Do not judge by appearances, but judge with right judgment.

Psalm 34 9 NIV Fear the Lord, you his Holy people, for those who fear him lack nothing.

Psalm 68 19 NKJV Blessed be the Lord, who daily loads us with benefits. The God of our salvation.

Psalm 9 1 KJV Praise ye the Lord, O give thanks unto the Lord; for he is good; for his mercy endureth for ever.

Psalm 106 1 KJV Praise ye the Lord, O give thanks unto the Lord; for he is good, for his mercy endureth for ever.

Colossians 2 6-7 KJV As ye have therefore received Christ Jesus the Lord, so walk ye in him: "Rooted and built up in him, and stablished in the faith, as ye have been taught, abounding therein with thanksgiving.

2 Chronicles15 7 KJV Be ye strong therefore, and let not your hands be weak for your work should be rewarded.

Psalm 33 11 ESV The counsel of the Lord stands forever, the plans of his heart to all generations.

2 Corinthians 9 7 NIV Each of you should give what you have decided in your heart to give, not reluctantly or under compulsion, for God loves a cheerful giver.

Proverbs 11 25 NIV A generous person will prosper, whoever refreshes others will be refreshed.

Luke 6 38 NIV Give and it will be given to you. A good measure, pressed down, shaken together and running over, will be poured into your lap. For with the measure you use, it will be measured to you.

Jeremiah 1 5 KJV Before I formed thee in the belly, I knew thee; and before then camest forth out of the womb I sanctified thee, and I ordained thee a prophet unto the nations.

Deuteronomy 6 6-7 ESV And these words that I command you today, shall teach them diligently to your children and shall talk of them when you sit in your house, and when you walk by the way, and when you lie down and when you rise.

Ephesians 6 4 ESV Fathers, do not provoke your children to anger, but bring them up in the discipline and instruction of the Lord.

Ephesians 5 1 ESV Therefore be imitators of God, as beloved children 2 And walk in love, as Christ loved us and gave himself up for us, a fragrant offering and sacrifice to God.

Nahum 1 7-8 NIV The Lord is good, a refuge in times of trouble. He cares for those who trust in him.

Psalm 27 14 KJV Wait on the Lord; be of good courage, and he shall strengthen thine heart, wait, I say, on the Lord.

Psalms 37 7-9 KJV Rest in the Lord, and wait patiently for him, fret not thyself because of him who prospereth in his way, because of the man who bringeth wicked devices to pass.

John 14 27 NIV Peace I leave with you; my peace I give to you. I do not give to you as the world gives, do not let your hearts be troubled and do not be afraid.

1 Corinthians 3 4 NIV Love is patient, love is kind. I t does not envy, it does not boast, it is not proud.

Ephesians 4 32 ESV Be kind to another, tenderhearted, forgiving one another, as God in Christ forgave you.

Proverbs 19 17 NIV Whoever is kind to the poor lends to the Lord, and he will reward them for what they have done.

CHAPTER 9

The act of making love should be a union between two people that is shared and guided by the heavenly father. It is not just a desire that is burning inside your flesh that makes you make a decision; you will regret all your life. Yes, you will regret it. If you are a female placed in a position since you are going into puberty. Dating and finding the ways of life, and can even be bullied into having sex with someone that you know nothing about or even the subject of this. Schools and Google are not the places to learn about sex and love. The churches should be able to guide you in the decisions of what our heavenly father desires for you but they do not encourage it. True education about sex comes from the home. From the parents. If your parents are not doing this, then of course, school education and whatever education that is stable, true and right, you should pursue.

God's word especially states how we are to hold ourselves and you do have value, my love. There will be many people entering your life, and some will sweep you totally off your feet, but what you do with your body is between you and God.

There is also the topic, that in having sex and engaging in this act, that both of you are so young that this act creates another human life. You yourself are just given the gift of life yourself and God has in store a wonderful journey for you and destiny ahead. Do not sell yourself short by agreeing to something that you do not really want or are ready for. It is a short-lived pleasure and a life time commitment from if getting pregnant. A lot of times, the child is not even able to speak for themselves. By abortion, adoption, and parents of the mother or father raising. This is not fair to the unborn child. You are not ready to make a decision like this. The best is to resist temptations and if the love between you grows and you are together, then that is something down the line you have endured and is lasting. This is in God's hands. Always go to him and pray about it. He will give you strength. No weapon formed against you will; prosper.

Even if unable to care for a child, there are many people out there that are not able to have children, and have, so much love in their hearts to give.

The avenue of what is best for all should always be explored. It does not make you a bad person. The love to be able to be given by another should be embraced. They are in a position to care for a child. They have been longing for a child for a long time. The unborn child should be considered and well thought out. Getting pregnant by a few senseless moments of lust does happen. Babies having babies. That is why, unless you are prepared, it is best to wait.

Even having multiple sexual partners and sex all the time is a call for the holy spirit crying out to you, to come to him. You are missing something here and need to ask yourself, why it is, that you are going from person to person. Most of the time God will reveal to you the answer for this. It is not an addiction, as it is flesh. It is not a replacement for a father that was not there, and you need to be held or comforted. That is a reason, and the need has to come before him so that it can be addressed and you can move forward with a healthy relationship.

Having multiple partners also runs a risk of catching diseases that last a life time. HIV, hepatitis, venereal diseases, herpes, and so on down the line.

Not all people are going, to be honest with you in the heat of the moment.

Guard your body as a temple of God. Once the chance you have given yourself to someone, you cannot get your virginity back again. It is not a game of chess to see who has and who has not. If your friend has had sex and they are trying to reach out to you, to have the same, stop and change the conversation in itself. Let God direct your steps and your life and you will be totally amazed. He has placed the right person in your life and you can rest assured of this. If this person truly cares for you and about you, they will have no problem in waiting or respecting your feelings. If they do not then it simply is not meant to be and most definitely not worth it.

I don't usually drop names, but in this subject, I am going to direct you to a pastor and his lovely wife that are fantastic in my opinion and whom I admire greatly. They are Steven Furtick and his wife Holly. They have a very blessed relationship and the story between the two of them is beautiful. Pastor Steven Furtick has a fabulous sermon on the unity between two people, sex, and relationships and he is the best as far as I am concerned on this subject. Take the time to get it and listen to it and hear it. You will love it I promise. In the midst of this always, always open your bible and go to the word. God will direct your steps. If someone is hounding you, pressuring you and constantly putting you down because you will not, continue to say no, and if this is not enough, then my dear, you do not need them in your life. If someone cannot respect your wishes, they do not and will not respect or regard you in any way. Respect yourself. Aretha sings it, r-e-s-p-e-c-t yourself.

God is full of victory and you are victorious. In the proper time, all will be added onto you. God has a union that is called marriage, that is between two people and the act of joining those two people in marriage. Holding onto and resisting your desires and coming together as two, as God intended, will be such a memorable experience that you will be glad that you waited. You can build an honest, godly relationship and walk together with the Lord. You can give the flip answer as to whether we had sex and still are together, yet, not married, however, do you want to get married? Since you have entered into a sexual relationship, is your relationship still strong? Has there been an effort to get married? You don't want to get married, there is no point in it? Here it comes blindly right at you. If, he or she goes out to fulfill their craving somewhere else and with someone else, that shows you that they will not be around and true commitment comes from within. Better to know now than later down the road, with children and upheaval you do not need. You should make God first and then all the rest will be added onto you. His love is lasting and unconditional. There is nothing in life guaranteed, but God will never abandon you or leave you on your own. He will always provide a way. Whatever decision or decisions you make, make sure you direct them to the heavenly father and wait upon him. A few minutes of pleasure is not worth a lifetime of unwanted measures. Taking care of a child, you were not expecting or equipped for. God provides the door if you will knock on it.

Marriage is a beautiful union between two people that develops. It does not happen overnight. What God has joined together, Satan is always trying to put under. It is the building of loving and giving, and if you are not ready for this, then stop, as God will provide the answer and answers, wait upon him.

1 Thessalonians 4 3 NIV It is Gods will that you should be sanctified; that you should avoid sexual immorality.

1 Thessalonians 4 4 ESV That each one of you know how to control his own body in holiness and honor.

1 Corinthians 6 19 NIV Do you not know that your bodies are temples of the Holy Spirit, who is in you, whom you have received from Gods? You are not your own.

1 Corinthians 6 18-19 NKJV Flee sexual immorality. Every sin that a man does is outside the body, but he who commits sexual immorality sins against his own body. 19. Or do you not know that your body is the temple of the Holy Spirit who is in you, whom you have from God, and you are not your own?

Hebrews 1 3-4 NIV The son is the radiance of God's glory and the exact representation of his being, sustaining all things by his powerful word. After he had provided purification for sins, he sat down at the right hand of the majesty in heaven. 4 So he became as much superior to the angels as the name he has inherited is superior to theirs.

Genesis 2 18 NIV The Lord God said "It is not good for the man to be alone; I will make a helper suitable for him."

Isaiah 34 16 NIV Seek ye out of the book of the Lord, and read, no one of these shall fail, none shall want her mates for her mouth it hath commanded and his spirit it both gathered and his spirit it both gathered them.

Psalm 33 2 NIV Praise the Lord with the harp; make music to him on the tin strings lyre.

Psalm 13 6 NIV I will sing the Lord praise, for he has been good to me.

CHAPTER 10

Setting goals and sticking to them. God has made a course for you to run and in making wrong decisions and choices, you may miss out on the destiny that he has prepared for you. If you have a position that you want and an occupation, do the research and time invested to see if this meets the life God has chosen for you and pursue it. Set goals for yourself and take a step forward into what it is you desire to do. There is nothing that you can't do. Each individual is blessed with a special gift and talent. In your heart, you will know if you are doing what it is that you are called to do. By his divine direction. If it is in your heart and you are doing it, you will find such joy and happiness that it just comes hand in hand. If you are struggling, it is not that you are failing at it, however, the good lord may have another place and something else for you to do. There is no true happiness in struggling every day and having no joy in what you do and are doing on a daily basis. It spreads over into your performance, your co- workers- your friends, and your family. God says, knock and I will answer, and God is the answer to the dilemma you are facing. It does not mean to automatically decide today, you are not happy and quit your job, school or leave your family. It is that in this, it is not meant for you, there is a better position waiting to challenge you, the field you are in, or the occupational that you are choosing. If in school, you should try and choose two to three positions that you would like to do. The one that catches you and you are good at, that is the geared direction you should go in. Also, be sure and enjoy school and the activities that school offers. Trying to be 21 and getting and wishing you are older, will happen. You can never get this time back. Each day is a gift and a blessing. God wants to give you an abundant life. Hand in hand you and him can "Do It". If you choose one and go for that which maybe all you can do, for right now, then be the best at it. God will add on to you, in his perfect timing. The relationship you build with God is everlasting and so surreal that you will enjoy each day waking up to him, and walking in his will. It brings joy to your heart and puts a spring in your steps. He will make your way known. When we resist, we are giving way to the devil to enter and confuse our destination and the will of God for our lives. Resist the temptation and he will be your captain. Set sail on an incredible journey and watch what he does with your life and in it. Build your relationship with him daily and watch it flourish and grow. You can do it. By now, you should be in reading the Bible daily, building a close relationship with God and you should open up your heart and believe that Jesus died for your sins. This is such an amazing gift that he gave to each one of us. God is so awesome and the gift he gave by his son dying on the cross, is indescribable of the pain he endured for us by shedding his blood for our sins. The nature of having a relationship with God, is so indescribable as to he is with you always, constantly and it should fill you daily of the love and the joy that he has for you. To even think about not wanting to be pleasing and obedient to him is beyond words. You can do all God created you to do. You can be all that God wants you to be. You can do all things that God strengthens you to do. Grace, grace, he gives to you. Cover yourself with his love daily. He is not a part-time father. He is from ever-lasting to ever- lasting. Not by power or might but by my spirit, you will succeed. Enjoy and embrace the course you have chosen and may God bless you in your endeavors. Carry with you day to day, "I Can."

Quitting does not do anything but rob you of the ability to achieve what God has ordained for you. In some situations, as to having to take care of a family member that is ill or a sibling, or even something that requires you yourself some time off, it does not need to be a permanent mark to not finish. That is in anything. Always try and do what you can. Do not live life with regrets. One turns into many more and before long, you are looking back and are filled with remorse, bitterness, and blame, and it poisons you and the life God wants you to have. Love God and yourself. We are all subject to events in our lives which make the times we are pursuing change and take a different direction. We do not have to be chained to those forever, as if given a sentence. We can accept those, turn them over to God and watch what he can do with them and for you. He most certainly does not dole out agony. If something presses on you daily, a loss, the pain, the hurt of someone did you wrong, and it plays over and over, immediately apply the word of God, over it, change your thoughts and think of something pleasing. Remove all related to the pain the moment creates, such as a picture, song, etc. Play some music, go for a walk, sing a song, hum, do something and before long, you will be on your way to peace and the relief of the injury caused. Memories are something beautiful given to us, and not all are happy. Receive them and enjoy all of them. Things do happen for a reason. Some have nothing at all to do with you. It has to do with the timing, the other person, and what is meant on your course that God has given you to do. It is not easy by far, and it can tear your heart into many pieces. You can do nothing apart from God and trying to isolate and separate you from the father and son. It is such an empty and defeating way to on top of take with you all the emotions you are feeling but destructive, not to have them, father and son, in your life. You "Can do it!". It is great to love, and you should, but when it is over, count it as all joy. It is over. God is the conductor in the orchestra and the music and love he plays is lovely and mesmerizing. Always remember the times, good and bad. Embrace them, and put one foot in front of the other. Are you reading your bible and seeing the changes God has in store for you? Each day becomes better and better, and you will see and feel a smile and love and happiness that is the best feeling to enjoy each and every day. It generates and permeates, you should be naturally starting to feel this now, as your heart is connecting to him. Life is short, it is but a flicker and before you know it, you are older and looking back. This time you develop in a relationship, with the father, you are realizing that he is the most important of all. Each day with someone, children, and all you have going on, are a true blessing as if in moments, it could not even be here. There is a grateful spirit that overflows onto others from inside you, that lets your light shine and unfolds the love of Christ and what you carry from within. Let that light shine daily and embrace the love he has for you. There is no age limit required, or is God Judging you. There is no time like the present to make that change and enjoy our heavenly father every moment. Ultimately you should be growing to know that our father is. He is everything that made you. He is everything that created the universe. He is the person that supplies all your needs. He is, he is.

Isaiah 46 10 NIV I make known the end from the beginning, from ancient times, what is still to come. I say, my purpose will stand, and I will do all that I please.

Jeremiah 1 5 NIV Before I formed you in the womb I knew you, before you were born, Iset you apart; I appointed you as a prophet to the nations.

Proverbs 19 29 NIV Listen to advice and accept discipline, and at the end you will be counted among the wise.

Proverbs 20 24 NIV A person's steps are directed by the Lord, how then can anyone understand their own way?

John 15 5 NIV "I am the vines; you are the branches. He who abides in me, and I in him, bears much fruit, for without me you can do nothing."

Matthew 19 20 NIV The young man saith unto him, all these things have I kept from my youth up; what lack I yet?

Isaiah 54 2 NIV Enlarge the place of your tent, stretch your tent curtains wide, do not hold back; lengthen your cords, strengthen your stakes.

Psalm 118 24 ESV This is the day that the Lord has made, let us rejoice and be glad in it.

Zechariah 4 6 KJV Then he answered and spoke unto me saying,

"This is the word of the Lord unto Zerubbabel, saying "Not by might nor by power, but by my spirit saith the Lord of host.

Romans 10 13 KJV For who so ever should call upon the name of the Lord shall be saved.

Romans 10 9 10 KJV If you declare with your mouth, "Jesus is Lord," and believe in your heart that God raised him from the dead, you will be saved.

10. For it is with your heart that you believe and are justified, and it is with your mouth that you profess your faith and are saved.

CHAPTER 11

Unconditional love is an experience that is non-wavering and is permanent. A person that you are in a relationship with should be showing love that is godly, and not with attachments of if you do this and if you do that, I will love you more. Love does not expect anything in return. It comes freely and from the heart. It is not selfish and expects things in return. God's love is pure and he will never desert you or leave you. He is always there and he knows what you are thinking and feeling. He does not have strings attached to his love. His arms are open to embrace you and comfort you always. If someone is pressuring you to perform and do this and give them this and that, they are nowhere near loving you as they do not even know how to love themselves. It is something that you need to keep your eyes open to and start to take things slowly, to see, if it is not just something that you, can do, for them. Love is not wanting your way and forgetting that the other person has feelings. Love is not threatening the person, if you don't do this or that, you don't love me, or, I am leaving, or you don't care, and on and on. That is control and no one needs that. We are never together that daily it is 100%. Some days, you may get 20% and they have 80%, but love is also understanding, caring, nurturing, giving, and being there no matter what for the other is love and part of giving love to one another. I hear you, is not listening and saying I feel you either. Being a part of the conversation and hearing and listening to them is the first step in communication. You cannot do everything and be everything for a person. God says not by power, not by might, but by my spirit, you will succeed. By God. Not by a person. God did not intend for us to be alone. The person you choose is not perfect, but in your eyes and your heart, love is. It is being there for them. Supporting them. In the good and the bad, being supportive and able to lean on them. It is building one another up. We are to surrender and be content in all things. Knowing that what it is we, are going through, God is there and will see us through. He has enough grace for each day, and we are to go to him. Seek him and his ways. A relationship without God is empty. When we express our love for one another, we have joy and laughter, and all falls into place where it is supposed to be and it works. Iron sharpens iron. When one is down the other lifts and builds the other up. A partnership indeed. When sickness or an ill parent happens, being there to take care of one another and being the shift for the presence. Giving and not taking, the same giving and not expecting in return. It is not selfish. Truthful and surrendering the truth of the love and foundation that you have with this person. Not misleading.

Faithful and not cheating or deceptive. Working towards the same goals and being on the same wave length as the other is on. When someone is always demanding their own way or ways, there is not anything you can do. You cannot change anyone, yet by being godly, you can be there for them.

We are to love one another and, as Christ loves you. When you get angry and say things, God knows them before you even speak them or act them out. Go to him, stop and take a breath and pray. As the heavenly father, what it is you are feeling and why you are responding as this. Are you owning your own stuff? It is easy to cast blame and blame another, however, the truth of the matter is, the other person, does not read minds, or predict the future. You need to see things in a new perspective and stand to own it. It is part of being mature and maturity. Feelings???

Everyone has feelings, about 100,000 a day. If you acted on every feeling that you have, you would be a basket case. What about what our father is feeling. He, sent his son into the world to preach the gospel, and he was crucified for it. What about when they threw stones at him? Was not enough that they, even cut into his side when he was on the cross, dying for your sins and mine?? Those feelings you have are only temporary, yet the son, is forever and he paid the utmost price. We all got stuff and we need to learn how to release it and let it go. Give it to God, and move on. He has no limitations to his love for you and me. If you are in a relationship, learn to love the person for who they are and not what you want them to be. Every day allow God to work in it and watch it grow. It is not going to be rosy every day, yet you can together be the team god made you both to be.

Love is something special that God has given to each of us, and each day is a gift. Enjoy the day and each and every day that God has given you to be with them and share those days together. There may not be a tomorrow and if you acted on your feelings, how would you feel for the rest of your life if you had to live with how you treated them or what you said to them based on your feelings?? It would not be very good to carry that stuff with you. Godly love is beautiful. You want to shine as gods light, so shines into the world and upon us. Joy is a feeling and a feeling that goes beyond any feeling that brings and drags you down. Try that feeling and share it and see, where it can take you. The things you two can enjoy are immeasurable and if you both have different likes and dislikes, can share both and have so much, to speak and share together. God created the whole universe, and if you are fortunate enough to do things, enjoy the beauty of what he created. The trees, the ocean, the continents, the actors, the artists, the musicians, the children of God, everything he designed, he designed for you, to enjoy. Start enjoying. Start enjoying your relationship and the people God, placed into your life. Someone who is different from you, is just that, find something to like and enjoy about them. Everyone has a special gift and a talent. Lift another up. In all things, acknowledge God. In all things.

There are also in a relationship that are two essential elements that go hand in hand. They are respect and space. Respect in that what they do and who they are belongs to the Lord. Sons and daughters, sisters and brothers, and thus and so. A spouse and partner, you see them as God sees them. Respecting them, not wanting to change, control and mold them into what you want them to be. Encouraging them and appreciating them.

Space, because smothering is not a decent quality. The time you spend with one another, no matter if it is 24/7 or a little while, time is precious and should be enjoyed and moving upward. Another is a person and loving them is not based on a dollar figure. If you have this or that. Love has no eyes to see the things a person possesses and owns. Love is and flows freely. Those are labels a person puts on another, and if that is what you want, then you should find someone who feels exactly the same as you, a lover of money. Two working together toward the same goals makes for a happy relationship, and just as easy as it comes, it can go just as quickly. God is the provision in all things. He will supply your needs. He will see that you are loved, and it is up to you to know in your heart that you are loved. Money does not hold you, comfort you, or does it solve anything. We want our bills paid, a home, and the comforts of what is normal, and we can achieve and work towards the goals of wanting more. God wants you to live an abundant life, and he wants to bless you. He does not want you to place praise and honor and worship on the dollar, as this will lead to unhappiness. You can have everything in the world yet not one day have any true peace or joy.

1 John 4 16 KJV And we have known and believed the love that God hath to us. God is love; and he that dwelleth in love dwelleth in God, and God in him.

Romans 8 35 KJV Who shall separate from the love of Christ? Shall tribulation, or distress, or persecution, or famine, or nakedness, or peril or sword?

Jeremiah 31 3 KJV The Lord hath appeared of old unto me, saying, Yea I have loved thee with an everlasting love; therefore, with loving kindness have I drawn thee.

1 Corinthians 13 4-8 NIV Love is patient, love is kind. It does not envy, it does not boast, it is not proud. It does not dishonor others, it is not self- seeking, it is not easily angered, it keeps no records of wrongs. Love does not delight in evil but rejoices with the truth. It always protects, always trusts, always hopes, always perseveres. Love never fails, but where there are prophecies, they will cease; where there are tongues, they will be stilled, where there is knowledge, it will pass away.

Ephesians 1 7 NIV In him we have redemption through his blood, the forgiveness of sins, in accordance with the riches of God's grace.

2 Corinthians 12 9 NIV To another faith by the same spirit, to another gifts of healing by that one Spirit.

James 4 6 NIV But he gives us more grace. That is why Scripture says, God opposed the proud but shows favor to the humble,"

Jeremiah 10 23 NKJV O Lord, I know the way of man is not in himself. It is not in man who walks to direct his own steps.

Philippians 4 13 KJV I can do all things through Christ which strengthens me.

Deuteronomy 31 8 NIV The Lord himself goes before you and will be with you, he will never leave you or forsake you. Do not be afraid, do not be discouraged.

Proverbs 27 17 NIV As iron sharpens iron, so one person sharpens another.

John 13 34 KJV A new commandment I give unto you. That ye love one another; as I have loved you, that ye also love one another.

Genesis 1 1 KJV In the beginning God created the heaven and the earth.

Philippians 4 19 KJV But my God shall supply all your needs according to his riches in glory by Christ Jesus.

John 10 10 KJV The thief cometh not, but for to steal, and to kill, and to destroy; I am come that they might have it more abundantly.

CHAPTER 12

Knowing Jesus as your personal savior. Do you know Jesus as your personal savior and the son of God? Have you accepted him dying on the cross, his blood shed for your sins? He is so amazing, and he is there for you to come to today, right now. He is not holding a score card, about the mistakes you have made, and he is not sitting in judgment, saying you are not allowed in. The things you are holding onto, he is ready to take and has already forgiven from you. Accept him into your heart and believe he is the Son of God and died and rose for our sins. He loves you, and the minute you accept him, your sins are forgiven and your name is forever written in the Book of Lambs. He knows your name. See, what an awesome God we serve and have. Enjoy the journey you have with the father and son.

Dare to walk hand in hand with him and see your life change.

Invite him into your heart and your life and watch the amazing changes daily that he does while walking with you. In all things.

To be baptized and cleansed, is a journey and starts with the king of kings.

There is nothing absolutely that is so horrendous that the heavenly father will not forgive and open his arms up to you to join and connect with his family.

Will you not today open your heart and ask the lord to come into your life? You will have a new beginning, and he loves you unconditionally.

Let God's light shine on you and watch the transformations he has in store for you.

When you are forgiven, your sins are forgiven, and you walk hand in hand with the father. Not to keep picking up the sins again. Deciding to follow the commandments and being obedient to the heavenly father.

God meant for you to have an abundant life and to prosper, not living broke down and a barely day to day life. Allow him to show you and every day may you make/bring your petitions before him and watch what he and only he can do.

Not worrying about yesterday and all the other yesterdays, and not about the tomorrows, as tomorrow is not here, but today. Today is a gift that God has given you, and you must be thankful for it, as you may not see tomorrow, and yesterday is gone and can't be relived no matter how much you would like to see it happen. What you want to say, could have said, would have said, make those the things you say and start to do today. I love you, thank-you, I am thankful for you, can I do anything for you, I am sorry, and all the things that daily need to be said, or not. Invest daily with building on something that is concrete. If ignored, the time can turn it into a tailwind and allowing/allows deception to set in, whereas bringing it to God daily and working on it, you are meeting it head on and placing it into his loving hands. He is our comforter.

Just because you are saved and have been forgiven for your sins does not give you an opening to go out and commit the same sins today all over.

It is opening up your heart and accepting Jesus as your personal savior and knowing that he died and shed his blood for your sins.

If you have seen me, then you have seen the father, he and I are one and the same.

Having eternal life with the heavenly father is awesome and in itself another gift from the father, giving his son as a gift to die for our sins.

That in itself is unconditional love.

Each day has enough of its own stuff, and to walk hand in hand with the lord, is a day, that you not alone. Rejoice in it and him.

John 6 40 KJV And this is the will of him that sent me, that everyone which seeth the son, and believeth on him, may have everlasting life, and I will raise him up at the last day.

Psalm 18 35 KJV You have also given me the shield of your salvation, and your right hand upholds me, And your gentleness makes me great.

Philippians 3 13 ESV Brothers, I do not consider that I have made it my own. But one thing I do; forgetting what lies behind and straining forward to what lies ahead.

Isaiah 43 18 ESV Remember not the former things, nor consider the things of old

John 14 9 KJV Jesus saith unto him, have I been so long time with you, and yet hast thou not known me, Phillip? He that hath seen me hath seen the Father, and how sayest thou then show us the Father.

Matthew 7 24 KJV Therefore who so ever heareth these sayings of mine, and doeth them, I will liken him unto a wise man, which built his house upon a rock.

Romans 5 8 KJV But God commandeth his love towards us, in that while we were yet sinners, Christ died for us.

James 1 22 KJV "But be doers of the word, and not hearers only, deceiving your own selves."

John 14 23 KJV Jesus answered and said unto him, if a man loves me, he will keep my words; and my Father will love him, and make our abode with him.

1 Peter 1 8 9 ESV Though you have not seen him, you love him. Though you do not now see him, you believe in him and rejoice with joy that is inexpressible and filled with glory, 9 obtaining the outcome of your faith, the salvation of your souls.

Psalm 4 7 ESV You have put more joy in my heart than they have when their grain and wine abound.

Psalm 5 11 ESV But let all who take refuge in you rejoice, let them ever sing for joy, and spread your protection over them, that those who love your name may exult in you.

Galatians 5 22 23 KJV But the fruit of the S, is love, joy, peace, long suffering, gentleness, goodness, faith, meekness, temperance; against such there is no law.

John 15 26 KJV "But when the comforter is come, whom I will send unto you from the Father, even the Spirit of truth, which proceedth from the Father, he shall testify of me.

John 14 26 KJV "But the Comforter, which is the Holy Ghost, whom the Father will send in my name, he shall teach you all things, and bring all things to your remembrance

1 John 2 2 KJV And he is the propitiation for our sins, and not ours only, but also for the sins if the whole world.

John 3 16 KJV For God so loved the world, that he gave his only begotten Son, that whoever believeth in him shall not perish but have everlasting life.

Proverbs 3 5 6 KJV Trust in the Lord with all thine heart, and lean not unto thine own understanding "in all thy ways acknowledge him, and he shall direct thy paths.

Romans 15 13 KJV Now the God of hope fill you with all joy and peace in believing, that ye may abound in hope, through the power of the Holy Ghost.

2 Corinthians 3 17 KJV Now the Lord is that Spirit and where the Spirit of the Lord is, there is Liberty.

Psalm 138 8 ESV "The Lord will fulfill his purpose for me, your steadfast love, O Lord, endures forever. Do not forsake the work of your hands?"

Acts 2 38 KJV Then Peter said unto them, Repent, and be baptized every one of you in the name of Jesus Christ for the remission of sins, and ye shall receive the gift of the Holy Spirit.

1 Corinthians 12 13 KJV For by one Spirit are we all baptized into one body, whether we be Jews or Gentiles, whether we be bond or free; and have been all made to drink into one spirit.

John 15 26 KJV Whatsoever I have said unto you.

Revelation 20 12 KJV And I saw the dead, small and great, stand before God; and the books were opened; and another book was opened, which is the book of life; and the dead were judged out of those things which were written in the books, according to their works.

John 6 54 KJV Whosoever eateth my flesh, and drinketh my blood, hath eternal life; and I will raise him up at the last day.

CHAPTER 13

A day of depression and being down on yourself is not a gift from our heavenly father. It is some confounded emotions set to ruin the day god has gifted you with. You are responsible for allowing the gift he has given you to ruin the day and the wonders of what he has in store for you.

It is understandable that we do not walk around joyful and exuberant every moment, as if we did, it would be a wonder if we were and are human.

Things get us down, circumstances, people, and life itself. It is up to us to embrace it and God, and as it is written, this is the day that the Lord has made, let us rejoice in it. Grab it, embrace it, and smile. It will all turn around, and nothing lasts forever, although it seems that it does. No one wants a joy stealer. If there is someone that robs you of your moments, separate yourself from them and what it is that is doing and creating this. Go back and thank God.

God is love.

Love has no conditions.

Now, that you have found what is causing you distress, deal with it.

Go into prayer and quietly come before God and ask him to give you the strength and grace to achieve success in the day.

He created all that is in the world and he wants you to enjoy it, him, and the life, he has given you. You are his child and you belong to him.

There is nothing in this world so important, so mesmerizing that it can take you. You can squash those feelings, you can control your emotions and how you react and respond, and you can get up and get moving.

Today make an effort to study God's words. Apply them. He will be with you every step of the way.

Rebuke the evil and poison and enjoy the time you have. We all get off to slow starts, and that is fine.

Promise yourself today, you are going to plant a seed to proceed.

Hand in hand, step by step, you can.

Psalm 118 24 KJV This is the day which the Lord hath made; We will rejoice and be glad in it.

Psalm 38 9 KJV Lord, all my desire is before thee, and my groaning is not hid from three.

John 14 1 KJV "Let not your heart be troubled; ye believe in God, believe also in me."

1 Peter 5 7 KJV "Casting all your care upon him; for he careth for you."

Proverbs 3 5 6 ESV Thirst in the Lord with all your heart, and do not lean on your own understanding. In all your ways acknowledge him, and he will make straight your paths.

Galatians 5 22 ESV But the fruit of the Spirit is love, joy, peace, patience, kindness, goodness, faithfulness.

2 Timothy 3 2 ESV For people will be lovers of self, lovers of money, proud arrogant, abusive, disobedient to their parents, ungrateful, unholy.

1 JOHN 4 17 18 KJV Herein is our love made perfect, that we may have boldness in the day of judgment; because as he is, so are we in this world, 18 There is no fear in love, but perfect love casteth out fear; because fear hath torment. He that feareth is not made perfect in love.

2 Corinthians 12 9 10 KJV And he said unto me, my grace is sufficient for thee; for my strength is made perfect in weakness. Most gladly therefore I rather glory in my infirmities, that the power of Christ may rest upon me.

Psalm 37 4 KJV Delight thyself also in the Lord; and he shall give thee the desires of thine heart.

Psalm 126 2 KJV Then was our mouth filled with laughter, and our tongue with singing; then said they among the heathen, The Lord hath done great things for them.

Proverbs 16 32 KJV He that is slow to anger is better than the mighty; and he that ruleth his spirit than he that taketh a city.

Ephesians 6 11 KJV Put on the whole armor of God, that ye may be able to stand against the wiles of the devil.

Proverbs 12 16 KJV A fool's wrath is presently known, but a prudent man covereth shame.

Hebrews 4 12 KJV For the word of God is quick, and powerful and sharper than and two-edged sword, piercing even to the dividing asunder of soul and spirit, and of the joints and marrow, and is a discerner of the thoughts and intents of the heart.

Joshua 1 8 KJV This book of the law shall not depart out of thy mouth, but thou shalt meditate therein day and night, that thou mayest observe to do according to all that is written thereof; for then thou shalt make my way prosperous, and then thou shalt have good success.

Psalm 119 105 KJV Thy word is a lamp unto my feet, and a light unto my path.

1 Corinthians 3 6 NIV I planted the seed, Apollos watered it, but God has been making it grow.

CHAPTER 14

The hurts, the sorrows. We all go through things that create a feeling of sadness. Some more than others. However, we can decide whether to allow it to poison us or to teach us to grow and have compassion for others.

To have to endure is not what the good lord wants us to do, he wants us to come boldly to him. He is the comforter.

It is so hard, yes, it is hard. There is nothing wrong with loving someone so much that you believe your whole world has ended because they left. God, wants you to be dependent on him and he wants you to know he is there.

Feelings do not have to take hold of you to where you allow it to rob you of your joy or your destination as to where God wants you to be.

Choose to accept the things that have come, as you do not have any control over them. What you have control of is yourself and how you react to them and whose you are.

Each day is set accordingly and we are to embrace and rejoice that this day as a special gift was given to you and me.

Debts, death, loss, agitation, all these have a place, and that place is not to rule or govern you. There is a time to mourn. The debt, he, will supply all your needs. Step by step, hand over hand, you will work through this, and he promises never to leave you. He is a God, of mercy, love, and plenty. Walk with him and watch him take you to your next direction, and pray. Thank the lord for all he is doing. You may feel like it is empty or alone, however, you are never alone. Turn to him now and ask him to restore you, his hope and his joy, his love, will engulf you totally.

Feelings pass. Don't let opportunities to pass you by, people that you could and should love pass you by. Enjoy the day God has given you. It is time to move on. He did not make us to hold onto the hurts and sorrows. He made us in the image of him. We will go through things. Holding onto him and his hand is the ultimate answer in all things and knowing he is. He is, so amazing. When you were down, he was there, when you were broke, he was there, when you gave birth, he was there, when you were born, he was there, when you got married, he was there, when you had your first fight, he was there, when you fell off your bike, he was there, he has always been there. Is it you that forgot? He is so amazing and life may throw things at you that you do not understand, but that does not mean that our Heavenly Father, has let you down or hurt you. It means, he is there with you in the transitions of all things, and most certainly, things are not always easy. Knowing that he has you in the palms of his hands and the comfort is there, is in itself an amazing thing. It is best to be still, rest in him, and know he has this, no matter what it is. The mess, or confusion going on in your head, is warfare to make you confused, tired, and overwhelmed, however, drop the negative thought and replace it with positive thoughts, and place your trust in him. You will see the walk and the love he has for you over passes all obstacles in your way. It is truly amazing. To even have a day without our father is a day missed and each day with him is wonderful as he is. Depression is an impression, and with proper care, diet, and exercise, it can be handled. We are not to understand all things and have all the answers. God knows everything and he will be there with you in all things. There is nothing to be ashamed of ever. The forces that come against you are forces that do not want you to succeed and to surrender to the father, actions of taking from you the gift God imparted to you with the birth of his son and also with the death of his son. Medically, being able to be treated has been given to people who suffer with depression and need the services of physicians, counselors, and such. Whatever it is that you need, he will most definitely provide the path and the way.

John 16 33 KJV These things I have spoken unto you, that in me ye might have peace. In the world ye shall have tribulation; but be of good cheer; I have overcome the world.

Psalm 51 10 KJV Create in me a clean heart, O, God; and renew a right spirit within me.

Proverbs 14 10 KJV The heart knoweth his own bitterness; and a stranger doth not intermeddle with his joy.

Psalm 118 8 KJV It is better to trust in the Lord than to put confidence in man.

Psalm 108 12 KJV Give us help from trouble for vain is the help of man.

Hebrews 13 5 NIV Don't love money; be satisfied with what you have. For God has said, "I will never fail you. I will never abandon you."

Mark 9 23 KJV Jesus said unto him, if thou canst believe, all things are possible to him that believeth.

Colossians 3 2 KJV Set your affection on things above, not on things on the earth.

Romans 15 6 KJV That ye may with one mind glorify God, even the Father of our Lord Jesus Christ.

Philippians 3 13 14 KJV Brethren, I count not myself to have apprehended; but this one thing I do, forgetting those things which are behind, and reaching forth into those things which are before.

Luke 9 23 KJV "And he said to them all, If any man will come after me, let him deny himself, and take up his cross daily, and follow me. Trusting God to double when faced with sorrows.

Isaiah 61 7 NIV Instead of your shame you will receive a double portion, and instead of disgrace you will rejoice in your inheritance.

And so, you will inherit a double portion in your land, and everlasting joy will be yours.

James 1 17 KJV Every good gift and every perfect gift is from above, and cometh down from the Father of lights, with whom is no variableness, neither shadow or turning.

Isaiah 41 10 NKJV Fear not, for I am with you; be not dismayed, for I am your God; I will strengthen you, I will help you, I will uphold you with my righteous right hand.

Zephaniah 3 17 KJV "The Lord your God is in your midst, a mighty one who will save; he will rejoice over you with gladness, he will quiet you by his love; he will exult over you with loud singing.

Psalm 62 5 KJV My soul, wait thou only upon God; for my expectation is from him.

Psalm 46 10 KJV "Be still, and know that I am God; I will be exalted among the heathen, I will be exalted in the earth.

Zechariah 3 2 ESV And the Lord said to Satan, The Lord rebuke you, O Satan the Lord who has chosen Jerusalem rebuke you! Is this not a brand plucked from the fire?

Ephesians 6 12 ESV For we do not wrestle against flesh and blood, but against the rulers, against the authorities, against the cosmic powers over this present darkness, against the spiritual forces of evil in the heavenly places.

2 Timothy 22 26 KJV Flee also youthful lusts; but follow righteousness, faith, charity, peace, with them that call on the Lord out of a pure heart. 23 But foolish and unlearned questions avoid, knowing that they do gender strifes.24 And the servant of the Lord must not strive; but be gentle unto all men, apt to teach, patient. 25 In meekness instructing those that oppose themselves if God peradventure will give them repentance to the acknowledging of the truth;26 And that they may recover themselves out of the snare of the devil, who are taken captive by him at his will.

Zechariah 8 12 KJV For the seed shall be prosperous; the vine shall give their dew; and I will cause the remnant of this people to possess all these things.

Matthew 13 37 KJV He answered and said unto them, He that soweth the good seed is the Son of man.

James 3 18 KJV And the fruit of the righteousness is sown in peace of them that make peace.

Mark 4 26 KJV And he said, So is the kingdom of God, as if a man should cast seed into the ground.

Psalm 126 5 KJV They that sow in tears shall reap in joy.

CHAPTER 15

Illness or devastating news regarding your health and wellbeing. You have just been given the news about your health that rocketed your world. What are you going to do? First thing is to go to your father and thank Him, that he is there with you. The next is to pray that he will inform you of all you need to know and do. To also lead you to a care provider that will care not only for you, but about you. You do not need to go through anything alone. With father and son, you are not alone. You are to be strong and of good courage. Certainly, it is not easy to be told you have cancer, kidney failure, or problems of any kind or of any magnitude. However, it is not a sentence that states, you are defeated, and no weapon formed against you shall prosper, you are to condemn it and know this is God's promise to you.

Believe and you will achieve. He loves you unconditionally, and he will never leave your side or you. Hand in hand, you walk together and you will see what the good Lord wants you to know. There is nothing wrong with being scared or afraid, that is a natural feeling. It is not easy, given a blow and not knowing the outcome. It is also not good falling apart and going to pieces because that adds nothing to it but creates more anguish for you. The peace the Lord gives us is a peace that says he has this. Continue to be happy, rest, and peaceful. Surround yourself with people who bring you joy, things that bring you joy, and do the things you enjoy. Even if it takes a while to do, you can enjoy and do anything that makes you happy and brings you happiness. Sorrow and self-pity will not bring anything to it, you have what it takes to overcome anything and by his stripes, you are healed. As the lord's prayer states, his will be done. Surrender unto him and walk with him. He will fulfill his plans for you. You are loved. Ask yourself if you are running around as a chicken without a head, what that accomplishes.

Being frantic is not an option. Nor alone. You are not alone, never. I love you too. Should you ever feel that there is no one there and want to talk or write, I will make every effort to answer all mail. Sometimes, we just need someone to listen to us and hear us. God hears us all the time even when we are just thinking and before it even became a thought, he knew what we were thinking. He not only has the answers, he is the answer. In all things. Don't rob yourself from an awesome relationship with the father and son.

Nor, let anyone else rob you of your joy. You can even, in going through things, step out and be a blessing for someone else or show an act of kindness. You have the day today. Make the best of it and embrace it and embrace him. You say you can't because of the pain, well certainly he will be with you, there in that also. Each step you take and breath you take, be thankful for and know he is there in all things, never desert you for one moment. It is not easy, my love, but you can be healed, you can be well and you can achieve all the lord has for your journey and that he wants you to be and that he has designed for you. Due to sin and sinful nature, we are all going to pass on. He has prepared a place for us, with him, that has no sadness, pain, or anything that is shedding darkness in this world. Today if you do not know Him, make Him, your personal savior, and ask and repent of your sins. He will come into your heart and be there and be the light of your path. You are not too old, nor is there a time table for his love for you.

Stop now to open your heart onto him and to him. He is an amazing father, the best of the best. Do not allow a devastating blow or unknown territory to damper or take from you, allowing it to take hold of you. Allow the presence of the holy spirit and God to transform you with his love, and know healing is from him and he represents love. Life and death come from the tongue. You can speak life into existence. Healing is from inside and speak it, and remain and be positive. No weapon formed against you will prosper!

Hebrews 4 15 16 NIV For we do not have a high priest that is unable to empathize with our weaknesses, but we have one who has been tempted in every way, just as we are- yet he did not sin. Let us then approach God's throne of grace with confidence, so that we may receive mercy and final grace in our time of need.

Romans 8 28 NIV And we know that in all things God works for the good of those who love him, who have been called according to his purpose.

Isaiah 53 5 KJV But he was wounded for our transgressions, he was bruised for our own iniquities; the chastisement of our peace was upon him; and with his stripes we are healed.

2 Corinthians 5 21 KJV For he hath made him to be sin for us, who knew no sin; that we might be made the righteousness of God in him.

Ephesians 1 7 KJV In whom we have redemption through his blood, the forgiveness of sins, according to the riches of his grace.

Matthew 9 35 KJV And Jesus went about all the cities and villages, teaching in their synagogues, and preaching the gospel of the kingdom, and healing every sickness and every disease among the people.

Psalm 30 2 ESV O Lord my God, I cried to you for help, and you have healed me.

Deuteronomy 31 6 KJV Be strong and of good courage, fear not, nor be afraid of them; for the Lord thy God, he it is that doth go with thee; he will not fail thee, nor forsake thee.

Joshua 1 5 KJV There shall not any man be able to stand before thee all the days of thy life; as I was with Moses, so I will be with thee; I will not fail thee, nor forsake thee.

Matthew 16 24 KJV Then Jesus told his disciples, if anyone would come after me, let him deny himself and take up his cross and follow me.

James 4 7 ESV Submit yourselves therefore to God. Resist the devil, and he will flee from you.

John 1 1 ESV In the beginning was the Word, and the word was with God and the word was God.

John 14 6 ESV Jesus said to him, I am the way, and the truth, and the life. No one comes to the Father except through me.

John 16 24 KJV Hitherto have ye asked nothing in my name; ask, and ye shall receive, that your joy may be full.

Psalm 8 9 NIV O Lord, our Lord, how majestic is your name in all the earth.

1 Peter 3 10 NIV For he that will love life, and see good days, let him refrain his tongue from evil, and his lips that they speak no guile.

Matthew 4 4 NIV But he answered and said, it is written, Man shall not live by bread alone, but by every word that proceedeth out of the mouth of God.

CHAPTER 16

Being alone is either something that you have chosen, or it is something that you are experiencing and will be at some time in your life. You are never completely alone, as God says he will never leave or forsake you. There are many times when it is possible to not have human contact. It could be that you are in a situation of being in a foreign country due to supporting a spouse, in the military, or have just recently lost someone through death, abandonment, or whatever situation may arise or occur. You may even have isolated yourself from socializing for short from taking stock in yourself and your goals. The reasons are not really what is the priority. It is that you see that something from this and the trials that you and I and others face are that which it is a time to grow, reset your goals, and develop a relationship with our heavenly father. A time to reflect. We do not often understand what it is that is going on. It seems that everything is coming out of the blue at once, and we do not understand. Sometimes, it is not for us at all to understand, but the divine direction of what our father wants from us and has for us. He has no desire to hurt, harm, or take from us. He is full of love, compassion and comfort. For all times and for all things. Actually, in building a relationship with our father, it is in this time also, you can see, that you are also able to do some things that you enjoy or even be led to try something new, that during the time you were not alone, you would never even try. Allow the holy spirit to flow through and work in you and ask the good Lord to direct your steps in all things. Do not allow circumstances to take hold and control you. Losing a friend, someone who walks away really does not mean anything. Treasure the time and things you did together and do not allow it to poison you. Certainly, if it is a death, mourn and allow yourself the time to grieve. Hurting, pain, and the absence of someone special in your life as a spouse, child and other is loss and a time to grieve. God is there with you every moment. Bitterness does not achieve anything and it is a pure poison. Yesterday is gone. The what-ifs don't mean anything, and tomorrow is not even here, so you cannot predict it or the things that come in tomorrow. Today is a gift, and we should all be grateful for it.

Thanking God each and every day for this new day and do our best in it. This is the day that the Lord has made, rejoice in it. It means specifically that. Rejoice. God will give you new friends. God will give you a spouse. It is in his perfect timing.

Your destiny was preordained before you were even born. It is up to you to

develop a relationship with the father and let him show you what you are to know and do. Surrender your heart and live unto him. It may be that you are going through things you don't understand, and you have done absolutely nothing to have them happen, or to suffer. It could be people leaving, friends, spouse, girl/boyfriend, and it could not be just solely one, it could be several or so. You might not understand why, but it is not up to us to decide or figure out why. Jesus said he has his arms open for us all to come to him and he has the

most divine love anyone could ever have, yet many have turned away from him. Now if that does not comfort you, and stop you from thinking about not thinking about yourself, then really look at it. You will get over it. The person that did walk away or hurt you wave goodbye to and be done with it. Life is too short to be pulling it around with you. It is a heavy weight that the good Lord does not want you to have or to carry. Whatever, let it go. Thank the lord you had the time with the person and pray for them. Loneliness is not an option; it is a choice. Call someone, get involved in a group, go visit someone in a nursing home, or a neighbor, join a club, in church, they have lots of groups, be a mentor, choose a hobby, go to school, exercise, do something. Sitting around moping is not what God wants you to do. One, you are allowing the dark to steal and rob you of what the good lord has planned for you. When a door closes, another is always sure to open. Our heavenly father is truly amazing. It is what we do when we are going through these things, that counts. We can trust and rest in Him, to know Heis our father, and He, knows what is best for us. You may want things right at the very moment and may not understand why there is not an answer to your time table, now time. However, He will be there at the appropriate time and He knows that time. Rest in Him. He supplies all your needs. Presently, you need him, seek Him... When a negative thought comes into your mind, rebuke it and cast it down, change your thinking, get up and move and do something. Do not feed that negative thought. Always something good is going to come from this. Allow him to move in you and to move you. Don't allow yourself and your life to be lived with whys, and pity, and regrets. We were not designed to live beaten down or adversely. Jesus came so we could know the father and live life abundantly. Being joyful and thankful.

Today, start new and afresh and give God the thanksgiving that he so richly deserves and watch the good lord change your life and you. Everything is a process and with each step you take He is there right with you. Holding you up and giving you strength for each day and each moment. Worship him, not things,

people, or money. All things will be added onto you. Loneliness, you are never alone. Smile and the whole world smiles back. Love and you will be loved. Give and you will receive. Share and sharing come's back to you in many ways and forms.

Deuteronomy 31 8 NLT Do not be afraid or discouraged, for the Lord will personally go ahead of you. He will be with you, he will neither fail you nor abandon you.

Joshua 1 5 NLT No one will be able to stand against you as long as you live for, I will be with you as I was with Moses. I will not fail you or abandon you.

1 Kings 8 57 NLT May the Lord our God be with us as he was with our ancestors; may he never leave us or abandon us.

James 1 12 ESV Blessed is the man who remains steadfast under trial, for when he has stood the test he will receive the crown of life, which God has promised to those who love him.

1 Corinthians 10 13 ESV No temptation has overtaken you that is not common to man. God is faithful, and he will not let you be tempted beyond your ability, but with the temptation he will also provide the way of escape, that you may be able to endure it.

James 1 2-8 ESV Count it all joy, my brothers, when you meet trials of various kinds, for you know that the testing of your faith produces steadfastness. And let steadfastness have its full effect, that you may be perfect and complete, lacking in nothing. If any of you lacks wisdom, let him ask God, who gives generously to all without reproach, and it will be given him. But let him ask in faith, with no doubting for the one who doubts is like a wave of the sea that is driven and tossed by the wind.

Job 5 19 ESV He will deliver you from six troubles; in seven no evil shall touch you.

Psalm 46 1-2 KJV God is our refuge and strength, an ever-present help in trouble. Therefore, we will not fear.

Isaiah 40 31 KJV But those who wait for the Lord shall renew their strength, they shall mount up with wings like eagles, they shall run and not be weary, they shall walk and not faint.

Hebrews 12 15 ASV Looking carefully lest there be any man that falleth short of the grace of God; lest any root of bitterness springing up trouble you, and thereby the many be defiled.

James 3 11 KJV Does a fountain send out from the same opening fresh and bitter water?

Deuteronomy 3 22 ESV do not fear them, for the Lord your God is the one fighting for you.

Habakkuk 3 19 NIV The Sovereign Lord is my strength, he makes my feet like the feet of a deer, he enables me to go on the heights.

2 Corinthians 9 8 NIV And God is able to make all grace abound toward you, that ye, always having all sufficiency in all things, may abound in every good work.

Psalm 37 4 NLT Take delight in the Lord and he will give you your heart's desires. This verse does not mean you will get what you want in every situation. But if your ultimate desire is a close relationship with God, you will always get that desire when you generously seek his will.

Proverbs 15 22 NLT Plans go wrong for lack of advice; many advisors bring success.

Proverbs 3 5 6 NKJV Trust in the Lord with all your heart. And lean not on your own understanding; In all your ways acknowledge him. And he shall direct your path.

Matthew 6 33 NLT Seek the kingdom of God above all else, and live righteously, and he will give you everything you need.

Psalm 37 5 ESV Commit your way in him, to the Lord; trust in him, and he will act.

1 Timothy 4 7 ESV Having nothing to do with irreverent, silly myths. Rather train yourself for godliness.

CHAPTER 17

Timing from God and his purpose is everything. It may be that you think you are ready and have everything in place, but God is not answering your prayers or meeting your demands. You are asking why? You want things your way and now. It is not now and it is most definitely not your way. You could sky-rocket to success and a star today or tomorrow, but will you really be ready for it and what it brings? Will you continue to honor God and grow in your relationship with him and will you be who you were created to be? You meet lots of opposition out there, called the beast. Someone or something is waiting to devour you. Robbing you of your relationship. Directing you to a path not chosen for you to take. God loves you. He has the best in store for you and the best is exactly where you are at right now, taking his hand and let him lead you to where you are to go. When he is ready. In his perfect timing. He knows better than you as to what is going to occur during this transition and before you even arrive at it. It is called god's blessings and he is the creator of the universe and will keep his promises. You must surrender unto him and worship him. Honoring and giving thanks for all he has done and is about to do. Always knowing he is working behind the scenes and is with you in everything. You may not be ready to take on the world, to turn from others' remarks, or to handle success and money. You might not be able to be overwhelmed and deal one on one with each issue, thus creating pressure. Where He has aligned everything in your course, walking along hand in hand with Him, on your journey. Timing is crucial.

God will let you know and thrust you in and towards what he, has created you to be and along with the gifts that He, has given you. Enjoy God and the journey. You must also be willing to not only commit yourself to him, our heavenly father, but commit yourself to do the best at all times. Not all good times arrive daily. We can look at them to happen and of course, keep our love and happiness focused on our father, but hard times come along with them, and it is how you respond to them that count. The key to happiness is not something found or explored, it is the decision to be happy and that is the key. God is true and wonderful happiness and it flows so fluidity from you that the peace you have should fly out to others. His will be done. Then of course, there is the flip side of this, and that is, if our father brought you this right away, would you think you do not have time for him, forget him, and fall prey to your adversaries? Would you stop building your relationship with him? There are many reasons as to why, you need to wait, and our father has the answer to them. You might need, say funds down the road for other things that were not present when you asked him about them. Like flat tires. A new roof, a trip unexpectedly. You are not in the position to know, what God knows, so rest in him and the proper time will establish and reveal itself accordingly to our

heavenly father's desires for you. He does not want to not bless you. He does not want for you to have something designed for your good, not given to you. He also does not want to see you get too big for the britches that you fly off the handle and think yourself better than others and to abandon him and your relationship with him. For sure, your gifts and talents came from and by Hm so you will see success and many blessings from our heavenly father. It also is not going to come at no effort from you either. One foot in front of the other starts success. Success isn't the many things you have or acquire either, as you will not take them with you. Or is it those that you leave behind? The best inheritance is that of love and our fathers' love which is for generation after generation and generation. His word and his love will live and be here forever. So next time you are wondering why not this moment, wait upon his timing and keep thanking God for answering your prayer in his timing and at his will for your life. It may take many years but don't give up on our father answering your heart's desires. Stand on his promises and know we walk by faith, not by sight. The spelling of frog is F- FOREVER R- RELY O- ON G-GOD. GOD is awesome. That is a little something to remember, I threw in. He has a perfect plan for you and his timing is the best. Keep on doing what you are doing and strive towards your goals, and in his timing, his answers to your prayers will be on their way. If not, it was not his plan for you. He may answer them immediately, or it may take many years but do not give up and especially, do not give up on our heavenly father. He is awesome.

Ecclesiastes 3 1 KJV To everything there is a season, and a time to every purpose under the heaven.

Habakkuk 2 3 KJV For the vision is yet for an appointed time, but at the end it shall speak, and not lie; though it tarry, wait for it; because it will surely come, it will not tarry.

Psalm 31 15 KJV My times are in thy hand; deliver me from the hand of mine enemies, and from them that persecute me.

Psalm 27 14 NKJV Wait on the Lord; be of good courage, and he shall strengthen your heart; Wait, Isay, on the Lord.

Lamentations 3 25 26 KJV The Lord is good unto them that wait for him, to the soul that seeketh him, it is good that a man should both hope and quietly wait for the salvation of the Lord. Honor God and grow in your relationship with God the father.

James 4 8 ESV Draw near to God, and he will draw near to you. Cleanse your hands, you sinners, and purify your hearts, you double minded.

Jeremiah 29 13 NIV You will seek me and find me, when you seek me with all your heart.

Colossians 1 9 14 ESV And so, from the day we heard, we have not ceased to pray for you, asking that you may be filled with the knowledge of his will in all spiritual wisdom and understanding 10 So as to walk in a manner worthy of the Lord, fully pleasing to him, bearing fruit in every good work and increasing in the knowledge of God. 11 Being strengthened with all power according to his glorious might for all endurance and patience with joy; 12 giving thanks to the father, who has qualified you to share in the inheritance of the saints in light. 13 He has delivered us from the domain of darkness and transferred us to the kingdom of his beloved son it in whom we have redemption the forgiveness of sins.14 God loves you and has the best in store for you.

Romans 5 8 KJV But God commended his love towards us, in that, while we were yet sinners, Christ died for us.

Romans 8 35 39 KJV Who shall separate us from the love of Christ? Shall tribulation? Or distress, or persecution, or famine, or nakedness, or peril or sword? 36 As it is written, For they sake we are killed all the day; long; we are accounted as sheep for the slaughter. 37 Nay, in all these things we are more than conquerors through him that loved us. 38 For I am persuaded, that neither death, nor life, nor angels nor principalities, nor powers, nor things to come, 39 Nor height, nor depth, nor any creature, shall be able to separate us from the love of God, which is in Christ Jesus our Lord.

1 John 4 10 KJV Herein is love, not that we loved God, but that he loved us, and sent his Son to be the propitiation for our sins.

1 John 4 16 KJV And we have known and believed the love that God hath to us. God is love; and he that dwelleth in love dwelleth in God, and God in him.

Philippians 2 13 NIV For it is God who works in you to will and act in order to fulfill his good purpose.

1 Corinthians 12 6 NLT God works in different ways, but it is the same God who does the work in all of us.

2 Corinthians 3 18b NLT And the Lord- who is the spirit- makes us more and more like him as we are changed into his glorious image. Amen.

John 5 17 NIV In his defense Jesus said to them, "My father is always at his work to this very day and I too am working."

Hebrews 13 21 NLT May he equip you with all you need for doing his will. May he produce in you, through the power of Jesus Christ, every good thing that is pleasing to him. All glory to him forever and ever. Amen.

Psalm 68 19 KJV Blessed be the Lord, who daily loadeth us with benefits, even the God of our salvation. Selah

Colossians 3 23 NASB Whatever you do, do your work heartedly, as for the Lord rather than for men.

Ephesians 2 10 KJV For we are his workmanship created in Christ Jesus unto good works, which God hath before ordained that we should walk in them.

Colossians 3 23 24 KJV And whatsoever ye do, do it heartedly, as to the Lord, and not unto men: 24 knowing that the Lord ye shall receive the reward of the inheritance for ye serve the Lord Christ.

Ephesians 1 18 KJV The eyes of your understanding being enlightened, that ye may know what is the hope of his calling, and what the riches of the glory of his inheritance in the saints.

Psalm 16 5 KJV The Lord is the portion of my inheritance and of my cup; thou maintainest my lot.

2 Corinthians 5 7 8 NKJV For we walk by faith, not by sight.8 We are confident, yes, well pleased rather to be absent from the body and to be present with the Lord.

Proverbs 16 9 KJV A man's heart deviseth his way; but the Lord directeth his steps.

Psalm 32 8 KJV I will instruct thee and teach thee in the way which thou shalt go. I will guide thee with mine eye.

Psalm 119 105 KJV Thy word is a lamp unto my feet, and a light unto my path.

Jeremiah 29 11 KJV For I know the plans I have for you, declares the Lord, plans to prosper you and not to harm you, plans to give you hope and a future.

CHAPTER 18

U nity, we have a choice to we can live as we want, and make decisions and give opinions as to what we want and fight for what we believe. However, are they in accordance with, and following the father's instructions and being obedient to his word? Changes and evolution are always going to come as selfish desires and ambitions. Honoring the lord and doing as he wants is the uppermost concern in achieving success at anything. We need to stop calling concern to color, or race, as we are all and were created by the heavenly father. If there was a time when you or I needed a blood transfusion and it was seconds to make that call, and because of some opinion you have towards a race, would it stop you from that person giving you blood to live? No. We are sons and daughters of GOD, and we are the same. We have different views and likes and dislikes, but the color is not something that is designed to fully absorb your life over. It takes so much a way and robs you of enjoyment. Enjoyment of meeting and knowing a child of God. It is so pathetic to think you would even waste one moment on a thought of prejudice. God created us to love one another and we must love all. The world is in turmoil and it is by selfish desires and ignorance that we continue to fight amongst each other and to fight for things that really do matter. If we surround ourselves with God and his desires, we can become a nation that thrives and grows. Unity is you and I, and we all need to become one nation that serves the lord, and cares about one another. One person, it says, can't make a change, but yes, one person and another and another can make a change for the better. When God is in the plan and is at the forefront of all concerned, he will see that it propels into the desired outcome of what it is supposed to be and established. If you go it alone and have ideas and thoughts that are not consistent with his desires and his ideas, it will be futile and quite possibly a direction in which you do not need to go in. There are too many things out there right now that make it almost impossible for a person to have or do. People today do not even want to do their jobs. Everything has become digital, and personal contact is almost non-existent, as well as communication with a person's own family. Instead of going to see them, they use Facebook, twitter, or anything that is social media, and they need contact. Smiles, hugs, kisses, to see their own family, children, grandchildren, and maybe even a personal letter, which has gone south. Sad to say, life is short, and the time it took to drive to a house to give somebody a hug was instead sent a fast hit on face book that said, hello mom, too busy. We need to take time for each other.

Even in checkout lines, you have a cashier that has a real chip on their shoulder and is doing you a favor to wait on you. Instead of reacting to their actions, we should stop and think that they are having a bad day or something is not right with them. Excuse the behavior and smile, and maybe even encourage them to unload the sadness to have a better day. Laughter goes a long way, and soon it passes off onto another. Or you could make them worse by treating them just as badly as they have treated you. God is in the circle of this, so let him be your guide. We are people that together can make a difference, and God will open doors to those that listen to him. We were not born with anything. Our opinions, and our beliefs, were all taught to us in some form or fashion. In the bible, it says how we, as Christ's children, are to act. God formed us and in the image of him. Instead of fighting because of color, race, or religion, we should be fighting to get along with one another and build our country into a better place. Not only for ourselves but for our children and their children. Lifting one another up. Putting our trust in our heavenly father. Wisdom comes from our father. Pray for it. Unite yourself in unity. Loving and serving our father and each other. Committing your work into His hands. The changes that are happening so rapidly in our country, are catching you unaware as to you are so caught up in your own self-opinionated state, unwilling to change. If you don't make an effort to change, you will be caught in future shock because you refused to follow the Lord's wishes, and change has evolved into such a place that you are in a time warp. Years have gone by and one day, you open your eyes and say, where has the time gone? Make a change today and step by step, you will see that instead of being part of the problem, you will be involved in the solution and the resolution. Participate. As long as we are reluctant to make a change or an effort, we are limiting ourselves from the provisions that the good lord wants. Many times, he allowed others to do as they pleased and for forty years, they wondered around in circles. Jesus came in the form of man, we were lucky to have such an awesome gift given, to come and shed his blood for your sins and mine. He washed the disciples and one he knew would betray him. No one is above another. Master served the servant and servant serving the master. Love surpasses all understanding. Everyone not only wants to be loved, we all need to love each other. Teaching and giving start with you and it starts with me. Pass the love and kindness on. Unity. Joining together and loving one another. Start today! God said you are all my lambs. If you base everything on prejudice and live for it, it will consume and over-take you. We should be willing to understand and hear one another wherefore the changes that occur makes for betterment amongst and for each other. For without it, there will be strife forever. The most extreme prejudice there was, is the crucifixion of Christ. He laid down his life for our sins. Dare I say, are you willingly to lay down your life because something does not agree with you, based on a feeling? Or are you able to come together with an idea, a format, a conversation that starts with you and another and another to compromise, agree, remedy, and change favorably the conditions and assertions that each care about and form a better place for one another? The decision and decisions are solely yours, and the good Lord can move you to where change does take place, and by the lord and the way and ways of the lord. Seek him and it shall be added onto you. We are to love one another. Love starts with me and it starts with you. This is the will of the Lord. Nowhere does it state we are to hate one another and this, in our country now, is about hate and self. Nobody wants to be told what to do and when to do it. All is self-oriented, and it should be directed by the hands and the will of God. We all have a responsibility to one another to stand and love each other and each one of us can do that. Step by step, hand by hand.

1 Peter 1 14 KJV As obedient children, not fashioning yourselves according to the former lusts in your ignorance.

Proverbs 10 17 KJV He is the way of life that keepeth instruction; but he that refuseth reproof erreth.

Joshua 1 8 KJV This book of the law shall not depart out of thy mouth; but thou shalt meditate therein day and night that thou mayest observe to do according to all that is written therein; for then thou shall make the way prosperous, and then thou shall have good success.

2 Corinthians 6 18 KJV And will be a father unto you, and ya shall be my sons and daughters, saith the Lord Almighty.

Hosea 1 10 KJV Yet the number of the children of Israel shall be as the sand of the sea, which can not be measured nor remembered: and it shall come to pass, that in the place where it was said unto them. Ye are not my people, there it shall be said unto them, Ye are the sons of the living God.

Galatians 3 28 KJV There is neither Jew or Greek, there is neither bond nor free, there is neither male or female; for ye are all one in Christ Jesus.

Romans 2 11 KJV For there is no respect of persons with God.

Malachi 2 10 KJV Have we not all one father? Hath not one God created us? Why do we deal treacherously every man against his brother, by profaning the covenant of our fathers?

1 John 4 20 KJV If a man say, I love God, and hateth his brother, he is a liar; for he that loveth not his brother whom he hath seen, how can he love God, whom he hath not seen?

Acts 17 26 KJV And hath made of one blood all nations of men for to dwell on all the face of the earth, and hath determined the times before appointed, and the bounds of their habitation.

1 John 4 7 KJV Beloved, let us love one another; for love is of God; and every one that loveth is born of God, and knoweth God.

John 15 12 NIV My command is this; Love each other as I have loved you.

John 13 34 ESV Anew commandment I give to you, that you love one another; just as I have loved you, you also are to love one another.

Romans 12 10 ESV Love one another with brotherly affection. Outdo one another in showing honor.

1 John 4 11 ESV Beloved, if God so loved us, we also ought to love one another.

1 Corinthians 1 10 NIV I appeal to you, brothers and sisters, in the name of our Lord Jesus Christ, that all of you agree with one another in what you say and that there be no divisions among you, but that you be perfectly united in mind and thought.

Galatians 3 28 NIV There is neither Jew nor Gentile, neither slave nor free, nor is there male and female, for you are all one in Christ Jesus.

Matthew 22 37 NIV Jesus replied Love the Lor your God with all your heart and with all your soul and with all your mind.

Galatians 2 20 NIV I have been crucified with Christ and I no longer live, but Christ lives in me. The life I now live in the body, I live by faith in the Son of God, who loved me and gave himself for me.

1 Corinthians 10 13 NIV The temptation has overtaken you except what is common to mankind. And God is faithful, he will not let you be tempted, he will also provide a way out so you can endure it.

Matthew 6 33 KJV But seek ye first the kingdom of God, and his righenious; and all these things shall be added unto you.

1 Corinthians 10 31 KJV Whether therefore ye eat, or drink, or whatsoever ye do, do all to the glory of God.

Romans 11 36 KJV For of him, and through him, and to him; are all things; to whom be glory for ever. Amen.

1 Corinthians 13 12 KJV For now we see through a glass, darkly, but then face to face, now I know in part, but then shall I know even as also I am known.

Romans 2 11 KJV For there is no respect of persons with God.

1 John 3 2 3 NKJV Beloved, now we are children of God, and it has not yet been revealed what we shall be, but we know that when He is revealed, we shall be like him, for we shall see Him as he is. And everyone who has this hope in Him purifies himself, just as he is pure.

Genesis 1 27 KJV So God created man in his own image, in the image of God created he him; male and female created he them.

James 1 15 ESV If any of you lacks wisdom, let him ask God, who gives generously to all without reproach, and it will be given him.

James 3 17 ESV But the wisdom from above is first pure, then peaceable, gentle, open to reason, full of mercy and good fruits, impartial and sincere.

Proverbs 3 13 ESV Blessed is the one who finds wisdom, and the one who gets understanding.

Proverbs 1 7 ESV The fear of the Lord is the beginning of knowledge; fools despise wisdom and instructions.

Luke 21 15 ESV For I will give you a mouth and wisdom, which none of your adversaries will be able to withstand or contradict.

Philippians 4 7 KJV And the peace of God, which passeth all understanding, shall keep your hearts and minds through Christ Jesus.

Joshua 1 9 NIV Have I not commanded you? Be strong and courageous; Do not be afraid, do not be discouraged, for the Lord your God will be with you wherever you go.

Jude 1 21 NIV Keep yourselves in God's love as you wait for the mercy of our Lord Jesus Christ to bring you to eternal life.

Psalm 36 7 NIV How priceless is your unfailing love. O God! People take refuge in the shadow of your wings.

1 John 3 1 NIV See what great love the Father has lavished on us, that we should be called children of God! And that is what we are! The reason the world does not know us is that it did not know him.

Romans 12 10 KJV Be kindly affectioned one to another with brotherly love; in honour preferring one another.

1 Peter 3 8 KJV Finally, be ye all of one mind, having compassion one of another, love as brethren, be pitiful, be courteous.

1 Corinthians 15 58 NIV Therefore, my dear brothers and sisters, stand firm. Let nothing move you. Always give yourselves fully to the work of the Lord, because you know that your labor in the Lord is not in vain.

Mark 10 45 NIV For even the Son of man did not come to be served, but to serve, and to give his life as a ransom for many.

Deuteronomy 10 12 13 NIV And now, Israel, what does the Lord your God ask of you but to fear the Lord your God, to walk in obedience to him, to love him, to serve the Lord your God with all your heart and with all your soul,13 and to observe the Lord's commands and decrees that I am giving you today for your own good.

Jeremiah 29 13 NKIV And you will seek me and find me, when you search me with all your heart.

Matthew 6 33 NKIV But seek first the kingdom of God and his righteousness, and all these things shall be added to you.

Psalm 34 10 NKIV The young lions lack and suffer hunger; But those who seek the Lord shall not lack any good thing.

CHAPTER 19

Forgiveness is something that is hard to do when someone has hurt or betrayed you. However, you have to forgive in order to grow and move on. God, will not hear your prayers if you have unforgiveness in your heart. Why are you holding onto this and even having it? Recognize it and mark it down. Feelings come and go all day long. Are you so golden that you are walking on water? Everyone makes mistakes. People say a lot of things that sometimes that they do not even mean. The most out of this is, that hurting people hurt others. You can even go, and others hurt you so much and so deeply without cause or justification that even when not understanding, if you go to the heavenly father and give it to him, you release it and let go, and He will handle it for you. Pray not just about it, but pray for them also. It may never even resolve itself, but you have surrendered it to Jesus and it is in his hands. Let it go. If you allow it to continue, you are feeding it daily and you are basically picking up a bottle of poison and hurting yourself over it.

Yes, you can't believe that person did this to you or even would remotely do it, but the fact is, they did. You have no control over another person, but you do have control to how you are going to respond and react to it. We are to love one another as God loves us. No one said you have to associate with them, engage in more, or even see the person again, but forgiveness starts with you and your relationship with God. It is not even in prayer, God, will you pay them back? We don't want any harm or hurt to come to anyone. He loved us so much that he gave his only son Jesus, to die and give up his life for our sins. That is an ultimate gift that no one on earth is willing to do, yet God did, and Jesus submitted himself on the cross to die for each one of us. Certainly, you can in your heart find a place to forgive anyone of anything. Money, things, desertion, and cheating, have no place in your life that it should consume you to where you can't even function without forgiveness. You can love and you can forgive. You are not doing it for them, you are doing it for yourself. Where you can move forward. Where you can be the person that our heavenly father has created you, to be. Bitterness and the likes do not have any place in your life or your heart. We may not understand, but we certainly can take a stand to allow ourselves the love God has given us to advance his kingdom and move forward. You can even say, it hurts, and they hurt me so badly. I do understand. I know what it feels like. God heals you and mends the broken-hearted. He collects your tears and knows your sadness. He is the comforter, and if you allow him into your life, you will know and experience his comfort and his loving embrace. There is nothing you can do without our heavenly father. He gives you strength and courage to face all things. Not some things, all things. He is with you always. Whatever the circumstance may be, God will make way for you. He will protect you. There are not answers to some as to why people act and respond the way that they do, but we are not masters at knowing, controlling, or fixing things either. God provides a way in all circumstances. You can start today by forgiving them. It even goes as far as to not carry something about yourself and live-in guilt of it. God forgives us and our sins. We are not meant to live and carry guilt and shame. We were made in his image and when Jesus died for our sins, he rose and sat at the right hand of God. He said, confess your sins. It did not say to carry them around for the rest of your life. It does not say go out and commit new ones today. It is that you are saved and you are coming to him, and in your heart of hearts are asking for forgiveness. When he says, you are forgiven, you are forgiven. Build on that relationship with him.

Take the journey God has in store for you and watch it grow into a beautiful relationship. One in which you may reach out to others. God does know your hurt. He does know your pain. Nothing is hidden from him, ever. We can't answer for someone else or as to why they did what they did or even have a reason as to the workings of someone in an action of hurting others, however, we do know what we can do to live a life obedient to our heavenly father. We all must stand in judgment one day. Would it not be best for you to know that you wanted the life Jesus wants for you? It also goes on to say, this is the day that the lord has made, rejoice in it. It does not say, this is the day, that I hurt you in it, drag it all around all day. Rejoice, he has a gift of a new day and a new start.

Enjoy it and him.

Colossians 3 23 KJV And whatever ye do, do it heartily, as to the Lord, and not unto men.

Psalm 16 11 KJV Thou will shew me the path of life; In thy presence is fulness of joy; at thy right hand there are pleasures for evermore.

Ephesians 1 5 KJV Having predestinated us into the adoption of children by Jesus Christ to himself, according to the good pleasure of his work.

Ephesians 4 32 KJV And be ye kind one to another, tenderhearted, forgiving one

another, even as God for Christ's sake hath forgiven you.

John 5 30 ESV I can do nothing on my own. As I hear, I judge, and my judgment is just, because I seek not my own will but the will of him who sent me.

John 5 19 ESV So Jesus said to them, Truly, truly, I say to you, the Son can do nothing of his own accord, but only what he sees the Father doing. For whatever the Father does, that the Son does likewise.

John 15 5 KJV I am the vine, ye are the branches. He that abideth in me, and I in him, the same bringeth forth much fruit; for without me ye can do nothing.

Isaiah 41 10 KJV Fear thou not; for I am with thee; be not dismayed; for I am thy God; I will strengthen thee, yea, I will help thee; yea, I will uphold thee with the right hand of my righteousness.

Isaiah 54 17 KJV No weapon that is formed against thee shall prosper; and every tongue that shall rise against thee in judgment thou shalt condemn. This is the heritage of the servants of the Lord, and their righteousness is of me, saith the Lord.

Zephaniah 3 19 NLT I will gather you who mourn for the appointed festivals; you will be disgraced no more. And I will deal severely with all who have oppressed you. I will save the weak and helplessness; I will bring together those who were chased away. I will give glory and fame to my former exiles, wherefore they have been mocked and shamed.

Romans 10 11 KJV For the scripture saith, whosoever believeth on him shall not be ashamed.

John 17 9 KJV I pray for them; I pray not for the world, but for them which thou hast given me; for they are mine.

John 3 16 KJV For God so loved the world, that he gave his only begotten Son, that whosoever believeth in him should not perish but have everlasting life.

Matthew 6 33 KJV But seek ye first the kingdom of God, and his righteousness; And all these things shall be added unto you.

Philippians 4 6 7 ESV So do not be anxious about anything, but in everything by prayer and supplication with thanksgiving let your requests be made known to God. And the peace of God, which surpasses all understanding will guard your hearts and your minds in Christ Jesus.

1 Peter 5 7 ESV Casting all your anxieties on him, because he cares for you.

Psalm 55 22 KJV Cast thy burden upon the Lord, and he shall sustain thee, he shall never suffer the righteousness to be moved.

Psalm 34 18 KJV The Lord is nigh unto them that are of a broken heart, and saveth such as he a contrite spirit.

Proverbs 15 1 KJV A soft answer turneth away wrath; but grevious words stir up anger.

Colossians 3 25 KJV But he that doeth wrong shall receive for the wrong which he hath done; and there is no respect of persons.

Romans 12 18 20 KJV If it be possible, as much as lieth in you, live peaceably with all men. 19 Dearly beloved, avenge not yourselves, but rather give place unto wrath; for it is written, Vengeance is mine; I will repay, saith the Lord, 20 Therefore if thine enemy hunger, feed him, if he thirst, give him drink, for in so doing thou shall heap coals of fire on his head.

Ephesians 4 31 32 KJV Let all bitterness, and wrath, and anger, and clamor, and evil speaking, be put away from you, with all malice.

Hebrews 10 30 KJV For we know him that hath said, vengeance belongeth unto me, I will recompense, saith the Lord, and again, the Lord shall judge his people.

Mark 11 25 KJV And when ye stand praying, forgive, if ye have ought against any; that your Father also which is in heaven may forgive you your trespasses.

Psalm 66 18 KJV If I regard iniquity in my heart, the Lord will not hear me.

Luke 6 37 NKJV Judge not, and you shall not be judged, condemn not, and you shall not be condemned. Forgive and you will be forgiven.

Colossians 3 13 KJV Forbearing one another, and forgiving one another, if any man have a quarrel against any even as Christ forgave you, so also do ye.

Matthew 6 14 KJV For if ye forgive men their trespasses your heavenly Father, will also forgive you.

Ephesians 4 32 NKJV And be kind to one another, tenderhearted, forgiving one another, even as God in Christ forgave you.

Revelation 21 4 KJV And God shall wipe away all tears from their eyes; and there shall be no more death, neither sorrow, nor crying, neither shall there be any more pain; for the former things are passed away.

Psalm 31 1 KJV In thee, O Lord, do I put my trust; let me never be ashamed deliver me in thy righteousness. Then came Peter to him, and said, Lord, how oft shall my brother sin against me, and I forgive him?

Till seven times? Jesus saith unto him, I say not unto thee, until seventy times seven.

2 Chronicles 7 14 KJV If my people, which are called by my name, shall humble themselves, and pry, and seek my face, and turn from their wicked ways; then will I hear from heaven, and will forgive their sin, and will heal their land.

Micah 7 18 KJV Who is God like unto thee, that pardoneth iniquity, and passeth by the transgression of th remnant of his heritage? He retaineth not his anger forever, because he delights in mercy.

Psalm 86 5 KJV For thou, Lord, art good and ready to forgive; and plenteous in mercy unto all them that call upon thee.

Proverbs 4 23 KJV Keep thy heart with all diligence, for out of it are the issues of life.

Jeremiah 17 10 KJV I the Lord search the heart, I try the reins even to give every man according to his ways, and according to the fruit of his doings.

Isaiah 65 24 KJV And it shall come to pass, that before they call, I will answer; and while they are yet speaking, I will hear.

John 17 22 23 KJV And the glory which thou gavest me I have given them; that they may be one, even as we are one.

James 4 8 KJV Draw nigh to God, and he will draw nigh to you. Cleanse your hands, ye sinners and purify your hearts. Ye double minded.

Psalm 118 24 KJV This is the day which the Lord hath made; We will rejoice and be glad in it.

2 Corinthians 5 10 KJV For we must all appear before the judgment seat of Christ, that every one may receive the things done in his body according to that he hath done, whether it be good or bad.

Matthew 12 36 KIV But I say unto you, that every idle word that men shall speak, they shall give account the thereof in the day of judgment.

CHAPTER 20

You are bored, this person gets on your nerves, you are offended, my feelings, me, me me me. Are you so full of yourself that you can't take responsibility for yourself, and it is always someone else, and they owe you, actually, you think, the entire universe owes you? Get over yourself and come to terms with the reality that the choices are yours, that you made. Did you go to the Lord with them before you acted? Did you seek His will before you responded? Did you look inside and ask the holy spirit to guide you to make good decisions? Did you wait upon the Lord for direction? Did you even stop for one minute and think about your feelings??? Feelings again come and go, and acting on them is not in accordance with his word. Period! Wait and let him be your guide. Accept and stand and own your own, own your stuff, yes, your stuff. People pay for the responses that you make, and life is not fair as to make someone suffer needlessly because of you pouting because someone did not dust your path with gold particles. It is called growing up, being mature, and looking to God for the answers.

Nothing is paved in gold but the kingdom of heaven. Unto God, we are to work, strive and live. No one owes anyone anything. If you did something for another, it is a gift of kindness, and unto the same in return, however, we can expect that they will repay or return, yet, do not do it with a heart of expectancy to recover and gain, profit off another. Out of love with no conditions, as the good lord has loved you and I, open up your heart and work from there. Freely, without resentment, disgust, or even threats. You cared in the first place and wanted to help, assist, loan, and be there, yet now you feel that they owe you. You gave someone a great gift of money and your luck has turned and now you are coming to collect, yet they don't have it to give back, you were there for them, and now they are not there for you, they hurt you, as you have done everything for them, and not received even a thank you. What was the purpose when you gave, did, and were there? Love, and to be able to help them, right? God supplies, all our needs. Not just a few, but all. As written before, in his timing. Wait upon the Lord, and you will see all his blessings and yes, you will. It is his will. It is by him. You are not God, and you never will be, so do not expect to do and think because you have done so many things that people owe you. God sees all that you do, and your reward is waiting for you in heaven, and he richly blesses those who have an open and flowing heart. He has no conditions on his love for you or I, so why are you placing conditions on anyone? Go inside yourself and deal individually with all that is bothering you and seek his will. He will lead you to where you, need to be, and in light of it, will show you the way in which you are to go. You will see that things will get better, you will find much happiness in letting this go and not carrying it along, and joy will return and be with you. Why sulk and be bitter all the time? It sure does not add to the situation and you drag the people around you down in it and with it. Half the time, the other person has forgotten it or did not know they hurt you. If that person simply does not care, you can write it off, still be there for them, or forget it and move it forward. You can only do enough and be enough for a person, if that person does not care, pray over and about it and release it and them into God's hands and care. You cannot control or be responsible for another when they have absolutely no concern about anything or anyone. Cut the cord, turn to Christ, and love them, care for them, but let them be out on their own!!

Romans 15 13 KJV Now the God of hope fill you with all joy and peace in believing, that ye may abound in hope, through the power of the Holy Ghost.

John 3 36 KJV He that believeth on the Son hath everlasting life, and he that believeth not the Son shall not see life, but the wrath of God abideth on him.

Proverbs 16 32 KJV He that is slow to anger is better than the mighty, and he that ruleth his spirit then he that taketh a city.

Ephesians 4 26 27 KJV Be ye angry, and sin not, let not the sun go down upon your wrath. 27 Neither give peace to the devil.

Proverbs 25 28 KJV He that hath no rule over his own spirit is like a city that is broken down, and without walls.

Jeremiah 17 9 KJV The heart is deceitful above all things, and desperately wicked; who can know it?

1 John 2 15 KJV Love not the world, neither the things that are in the world. If any man love the world, the love of the Father is not in him.

1 Corinthians 3 16 KJV Know ye not that ye are the temple of God, and that the spirit of God, and that the spirit of God dwelleth in you.

Psalm 40 3 KJV And he hath put a new song in my mouth, even praise unto our God, many shall see it, and fear, and shall trust in the Lord.

Romans 8 26 KJV Likewise the Spirit also helpeth our infirmities; for we know not what we should pray for as we ought, but the Spirit itself maketh intercession for us with groanings which cannot be uttered.

Isaiah 30 18KJV Therefore the Lord longs to be gracious to you, And therefore he waits on high to have compassion on you. For the Lord is a God of justice. How blessed are all those who long for him.

1 Timothy 2 1 KJV I exhort therefore, that, first of all, supplications, prayers, intercessions, and giving of thanks, be made for all men.

Ephesians 6 18 KJV Praying always with all prayer and supplication in the Spirit, and watching there unto with all perseverance and supplication for all saints.

John 14 13 KJV And whatsoever ye shall ask in my name, will I do, that the Father may be glorified in the Son.

Ephesians 4 32 KJV And be ye kind one to another tenderhearted, forgiving one another, even as God for Christ's sake hath forgiven you.

1 John 4 20 21 KJV If a man say, I love God, and hateth his brother, he is a liar, for he that loveth not his brother whom he hath seen, how can he love God whom he hath not seen?

Romans 12 18 KJV If it be possible, as much as lieth in you, live peaceably with all men.

1 Peter 2 17 KJV Honour all men, Love the brotherhood. Fear God, Honour the King.

1 John 4 9 10 KJV In this was manifested the love of God toward us, because that God sent him his only begotten Son into this world, that we might live through him. Herein is love, not that he loved us, and sent his Son to be the propitiation for our sins.

1 Corinthians 13 4 7 KJV Charity suffereth long and is kind, charity envieth not, charity vaunted not itself, is not puffed up. 5 Do not behave itself unseemly seeketh not her own, is not easily provoked, thinketh no evil. 6 Rejoiceth not in iniquity but rejoiceth in the truth.7 Beareth all things, believeth all things, hopeth all things, endureth all things.

Jeremiah 31 3 KJV The Lord hath appeared of old unto me, saying, Yea I have loved thee with an everlasting love, therefore with loving kindness have I drawn thee.

Ephesians 2 8 KJV For by grace are ye saved through faith, and that not of yourselves, it is the gift of God.

Philippians 4 19 KJV But my God shall supply your need according to his riches in glory by Christ Jesus.

Psalm 37 4 KJV Delight thyself also in the Lord, and he shall give thee the desires of thine heart.

Psalm 68 18 KJV Blessed be the Lord who daily loadeth us with benefits, even the God of our salvation. Selah.

Psalm 27 14 KJV Wait on the Lord, be of good courage, and he shall strengthen thine heart; wait, I say on the Lord.

Isaiah 40 31 KJV But they that wait upon the Lord shall renew their strength, they shall mount up with wings as eagles, they shall run, and not be weary, and they shall walk, and not faint.

Galatians 2 20 KJV I am crucified with Christ; never the less I live, yet not I, but Christ liveth in me, and the life which I now live in the flesh I live by the faith of the Son of God, who loved me, and gave himself for me.

1 John 3 2 KJV Beloved, now are we the Sons of God, and it doth not yet appear what we shall be; but we know that, when he shall appear, we shall be like him, for we shall see him as he is.

Psalm 37 9 KJV For evildoers shall be cut off, but those that wait upon the Lord, they shall inherit the earth.

Romans 12 15 KJV Rejoice with them that do rejoice, and weep with them that weep.

Psalm 55 22 KJV Cast thy burden upon the Lord, and he shall sustain thee, he shall never suffer the righteous to be moved.

1 Peter 5 7 KJV Casting all your care upon him, for he careth for you.

Proverbs 15 19 The way of the slothful (man is) as an hedge of thorns, but the way of the righteous (is) made plain.

Romans 12 11 KJV Not slothful in business, fervent in spirit; serving the Lord.

Hebrews 6 12 KJV That ye be not slothful, but followers of them who through faith and patience inherit the promises.

CHAPTER 21

Family, is something that is uniquely special and you should always recognize it for such. A grandparent is someone and something that is special and vital. Same with mother and father, sister and brother. Even without all the connections, a one-parent home, is also special. God chooses who he places you in a home with, and we are not meant to be alone and void companionship. There are always roots in a family, and there is no book on how to be a parent. You either have the Waltons or the Walnuts, and it is up to you to keep that connection going and alive and growing. We are all in god's family and a part of Him. To allow someone control over who you can see and who you can talk to and visit with is not an option for any relationship. A person that tells you, you can't speak to your family and is an outpouring of dictatorship, and control is not really someone you want to be connected to or with. It is someone that has no ability for human kindness. If you have had a disagreement and asked a person to forgive you even if there is no reason for the request, and it is a gesture to establish a relationship, then you have done what is required by God, and he will be sure to handle the person on the other side, not forgiving you. God is everywhere and knows all, and you, doing your part, is something that is obedient unto Christ. Family is forever and no one can take another's family from them. Anyone making such a request or command is unsecured and the only answer is no. No, I will not succumb to the desires of your request to snub and turn on my family. No, I may not agree with them, and vice versa, however, this is my family and/or for whatever reason, I will always love them and be there for them. We need to listen to them, just as God listens to us. Pray about it and keep being positive. If there is a valid reason, then you can look for the outside help that the person needs and assist them. A person has to want help and nobody can force anyone to do anything. God has control over everything and we have been given the free will to make the right choices. If in doubt, go to your bible, kneel down and speak and pray to the almighty Father and wait upon him, not seeking your own will, but He will be done! Casting blame is also not an option. You choose what you think, feel, and do. It is because of a choice you individually made, and did you consult the heavenly father and or concern him in any of it? It is your fault putting it on the parent is so immature and futile. The parent, whether it be one or both did the best they could at what they had and what they knew and is time to get over yourself. One day, your parent may not be here. Today is the day you are gifted with. Pick up the phone and call them. Tell them you love them. Want nothing back. God loves his flock.

Exodus 20 12 KJV Honour thy father and mother; that thy days may be long upon the land which the Lord thy God giveth thee.

Genesis 2 24 KJV Therefore shall a man leave his father and his mother, and shall cleave unto his wife and they shall be one flesh.

Joshua 24 15 KJV And if it seem evil unto you to serve the Lord, choose you this day whom ye will serve; whether the gods which your father served that were on the other side of the flood, or the gods of the Amorites, in whose land ye dwell, but as for me and my house, we will serve the Lord.

Ephesians 3 14 15 KJV For this cause I bow my knees unto the father of our Lord Jesus Christ.15 of whom the whole family in heaven and earth is named.

Proverbs 6 20 KJV My son, keep thy father's commandment, and forsake not the law of thy mother.

Psalm 138 8 KJV The Lord will perfect that which concerned me;

thy mercy, O Lord, endureth for ever; forsake not the works of thine own hands.

1 Peter 5 7 ESV Casting all your anxieties on him, because he cares for you.

Romans 12 2 ESV Do not be conformed to this world, but be transformed by the renewal of your mind, that by testing you may discern what is the will of God, what is good and acceptable and perfect.

Deuteronomy 32 7 KJV Remember the days of old, consider the years of many generations, ask thy father, and he will shew thee, thy elders, and they will tell thee.

Psalm 145 4 KJV One generation shall praise thy works to another, and shall declare thy mighty acts.

Psalm 103 17 KJV But the mercy of the Lord is from everlasting to ever lasting upon them that fear him, and his righteousness unto children's children.

Genesis 2 18 KJV And the Lord God said, It is not good that the man should be alone; I will make him an help meet for him.

Psalm 34 18 KJV The Lord is nigh unto them that are of a broken heart; and saveth such as be of contrite spirit.

Ecclesiastes 4 9 10 KJV Two are better than one; because they have a good reward for their labour.

1 Corinthians 1 10 KJV Now I beseech you, brethren, by the name of our Lord Jesus Christ, that ye all speak the same thing, and that there be no divisions among you, but that ye be perfectly joined together in the same mind and in the same judgment.

Psalm 133 1 KJV Behold, how God and how pleasant it is for brethren to dwell together in unity.

Proverbs 6 20 KJV My son, keep thy father's commandment, and forsake not the law of thy mother.

Romans 16 17 18 ESV I appeal to you brothers, to watch out for those who cause divisions and create obstacles contrary to the doctrine that you have been taught; avoid them. For such persons do not serve our Lord Christ, but their own appetites and by smooth talk and flattery they deceive the hearts of the naïve.

2 Timothy 3 1 5 ESV But understand this, that in the last days there will come times of difficulty. For people will be lovers of self, lovers of money, proud, arrogant, abusive, disobedient, to parents, ungrateful, unholy, heartless, unappeasable, slanderous, without self-control, brutal, not loving good, treacherous, reckless, swollen with conceit, lovers of pleasure rather than love lovers of God, having the appearance of godliness, but denying its power. Avoid such people.

1 Timothy 5 8 ESV But if anyone does not provide for his relatives, and especially for members of his household he has denied the faith and is worse than an unbeliever.

Ephesians 6 1 3 KJV Children, obey your parents in the Lord; for this is right.

Exodus 20 1 12 KJV Honour thy father and thy mother; that thy days may be long upon the land which the Lord thy God giveth thee.

Proverbs 30 17 KJV The eye that mocketh at his father, and despiseth to obey his mother, the ravens of the valley shall pick it out, and the young eagles shall eat it.

Ephesians 2 19 22 KJV Now therefore ye are no more strangers and foreigners but fellow citizens with the saints, and of the household of God.

Galatians 6 10 KJV As we have therefore opportunity, let us do good unto all men, especially unto them who are of the household of faith.

Romans 12 5 KJV So we, being many are one body in Christ, and every one members one of another.

Corinthians 12 26 KJV For we are labourers together with God; ye are God's husbandry, ye are God's building.

Genesis 2 24 KJV Therefore shall a man leave his father and his mother and shall cleave unto his wife; and they shall be one flesh.

Proverbs 12 4 KJV A virtuous woman is a crown to her husband; But she that maketh ashamed is as rottenness in his bones.

Matthew 18 21 22 KJV Then came Peter to him, and said, Lord, how oft shall my brother sin against me, and I forgive him? Till seven times? 22 Jesus saith unto him; I say not unto thee until seven times but, until seventy times seven.

Psalm 32 1 KJV Blessed is he whose transgression is forgiven, whose sin is covered.

Luke 6 31 KJV And as ye would that men should do to you, do ye also to them likewise.

Proverbs 24 17 KJV Rejoice not when thine enemy falleth, and let not thine heart be glad when he stumbleth.

Romans 15 1 2 KJV We then that are strong ought to bear the infirmities of the weak, and not to please ourselves.

James 2 1 KJV My brethren, have not the faith of our Lord Jesus Christ, the Lord of glory, with respect of person's.

Ephesians 6 1 KJV Children obey your parents in the Lord for this is right. 2 Honour thy father and mother, which is the first commandment with promises; 3 That it may be well with thee, and thou mayest live long on the earth.

Proverbs 15 3 KJV The eyes of the Lord are in every place, beholding the evil and the good.

Psalm 139 1 KJV Lord you have examined me and know all about me.

Isaiah 58 13 KJV If thou turn away thy foot from the sabbath, from doing thy pleasure on my holy day; and call the sabbath a delight, the holy of the Lord, honorable; and shall honour him, not doing thine own ways, nor finding thine own pleasure, nor speaking thine own words.

Psalm 133 1 KJV Behold, how good and how pleasant it is for brethren to dwell together in unity.

Genesis 18 19 KJV For I know him, that he will command his children and his household after him, and they shall keep the way of the Lord, to do justice and judgment, that the Lord may bring upon Abraham that which he hath spoken of him.

1 John 4 7 8 KJV Beloved, let us love one another; for love is of God; and every one that loveth is born of God, and knoweth, God. He that loveth not knoweth not God, for God is love.

John 10 11 KJV I am the good shepherd; the good shepherd- giveth his life for the sheep.

CHAPTER 22

Today our society is broken by a lot of different diversities and it may be called prejudice, it may be called depression, or anxiety, but there are a lot of hurting people out there. Wanting and desiring their own ways/their own will. We are all guilty of this. Prejudice is not something we are born with, it is something learned, picked up, or drilled into us. It is up to us as individuals to lay those thoughts down and not let anyone place their beliefs onto and into us. It is up to you to decide what is real, true, and correct and stand for a change. One person, yes, can make a difference. United we stand and divided we fall. Our heavenly father has a calling for each one of us. It is not designed by race, color, or creed. Rich or poor. There is not anyone that is better than you, and you, are not better than anyone else. We can drive to make that change standing together. The prejudice exists that we crucified Christ, and he paid the ultimate cost for our sins, and in that, he bore up everything on the cross. We are to be obedient to Him and do our Father's will. That is to love one another. If you see your brother or sister suffering, go to them, and reach out. In life they say, people have addictions. Now a classy way to make funds off of hurting people and labeling them. It is a person who is hurting and maybe they just, want to be listened to and heard, hugged, and held, knowing that someone just cares. You can either be the person there who cares or on the other side hurting, but you can reach out regardless and know Christ is there and he will comfort you. Nothing lasts forever. If we feel this disease and yes, prejudice is to a disease, we will have no cure for it. There is a well-known song out that says, "Make that Change." We can dare to sit down and talk, we can dare to stand hand in hand across the world, we can hug, love and welcome another alongside another, and most of all, we can stand united in God and let him guide and be the master of our paths and our destiny. Life is most definitely too short to bare up a cross you or I am not prepared to carry. Christ, again, died for our sins. We are to sing songs of praise and rejoice and be glad in the gift of the day that God has gifted us with. If your destiny is to unite, conquer, and bring together, then God will direct your steps, and we, can join in to be one country not divided but in union together to love one another. Let not color be a barrier for you not to know another person, as you are robbing yourself of a gift the good Lord has given you. It is called a friend, a brother, a sister, a mother, a father. Most of all, it is called LOVE! A child of God. There are many great people out there and they have affected the world in a profound way. You have Rosa Parks, who took a stand and as a lady, she moved to the front of the bus.

Not only Rosa moving to the front, but moving forward and making a change. You have Miya Angelou, a very profound and enunciated lady that has the wisdom of words that you would just dream to be able to absorb everything she said. You have Martin Luther King, another great man taking a stand to care about humanity. Mother Teresa, who gave and worked to help all, wanted nothing in return but to serve Christ. The list goes on and on of every culture and color to contribute to our world and bring peace to it, and we as individuals can also do this without violence, destruction, and murder. There will always be someone in the group or crowd that will not get along, agree, fight, and not stand because it is evil and the principalities of evil will exist on the earth and for a lifetime, as it is written, however, we can choose to ignore those who do not want world peace and try to show them as examples of living a Christian life that joy is just that. Putting an end to prejudice, putting an end to hate and hatred.

Putting an end to violence and murder. There are many ways in which God will lead you and the right path to take. Surrender it onto Him and let Him direct your steps. He will not only lead you down that path, he will also place the right people and everything you need, to do what you are called to do. Everything takes time and patience. We are not to be anxious about anything. If you stumble it does not mean that you are a failure, you keep on keeping on and he will be there with you every step of the way, every day. For now and always. Now there is this pan-epidemic which was not ongoing when I started writing. The pain and loss of anyone is shattering to say the least, yet so evil and inhumane to watch an officer kill another man. Yes, man, a human being, a brother, someone's father, son. Taking a human life. We, as children of God come together to stand for what the good lord has stated in the ten commandments, thy shall not kill. Taking a united stand to protect the rights of one another. Removing statues is not doing this and changing names is not doing this. It is anger that is spurring this on and not anywhere near a resolution in trying to make things right. A reformation act to all justice and how people are treated is what needs to change in all formats. A direct approach that will bring unity and the rights to all created and implemented into an order. It is not with law enforcement, it is seen in all areas of law, and those changes need to be incorporated and adopted. It is all people that are met with opposition as opposed to some who are able to buy their way out, and corruption does exist. We as a nation need to come together and talk about ways in which we as a whole can become better and rise up over indiscretions, and further each other. God says iron sharpens iron; we lift one another up. Our opinions are not always going to be the same, yet we should be able to speak and hear one another. Violence and brash words are not going to do this. Refusal to represent, ignore, admonish is not going to do this, and most certainly, changing a box of rice's name is not going to do this, or destroying a statue, which is made of clay. People before us, our ancestors, lived through all these events and rose above them, setting a path in which our country was created. Trying to make it better for us. Each and every one of us. We are to take what is and has been given to us and count it as a blessing, and move forward to the betterment of each and every person, with the goal of having better in our country and love between us. God says we are to love one another and the greatest gift is love. We can sit down and talk, have discussions, hold meetings and resolve the issues at hand and make things work right. It does not take violence. It does not take guns. Before long, there will be an entire world of vigilantes out, and nothing will be resolved. Our father says "my will be done; my ways are higher than your ways." Trust in him, our heavenly father. Pray and prayers towards his will be done. Take his hand, depend on him and in everything try to move forward. Regression, moving backward is not going anywhere. Appreciate one another, see one another, hear one another and love one another.

Some people are simply not going to change and hear you, but that does not mean you do not keep on trying. There are two sides, good and evil, just as in the Garden of Eden. Choose the right path and make a difference that honors the father and directed by the father. Do not let prejudice rule you. Look inside and make that change. Hand to hand across the land- lands. Let the good lord rule your heart and promote love and peace.

Everything belongs to the lord and it is all his. He will direct your steps. Are we not better than dogs? Dogs can see no color and love unconditionally. Barriers make for the inability and ability to know one another and enjoy one another. Everyone is special and has a talent. The heavenly father has placed something unique in each and every one of us and has placed in all of us love. Meet someone and appreciate and enjoy them. As the son opened his arms to all and said whoever knocks, I will open, do the same.

Make a difference and a positive change.

Luke 9 10 KJV So I say to you, ask and it will be given to you, seek, and you will find, knock, and it will be opened to you. For every one who asks, receives, and he who seeks, finds, and to him who knocks, it will be opened.

Deuteronomy 10 19 KJV Love ye therefore the stranger for ye were strangers in the land of Egypt.

1 John 4 7 8 KJV Beloved, let us love one another; for love is of

God; and every one that loveth is born of God, and knoweth God. He that loveth not knoweth not God, for God is love.

Romans 13 8 KJV Owe no man anything, but to love one another; for he that loveth another hath fulfilled the law.

Philippians 2 3 KJV Let nothing be done through strife or vain glory; but in lowliness of mind let each esteem other better than themselves.

Proverbs 18 16 KJV A man's gift maketh room for him, and bringeth him before great men.

James 1 17 KJV Every good gift and every perfect gift is from above, and cometh down from the Father of lights, with whom is no variableness, neither shadow of turning.

Peter 4 10 KJV As every man hath received the gift, even so minister the same one to another, as good stewards of the manifold grace of God.

1 Timothy 4 14 KJV Neglect not the gift that is in thee, which was given thee by prophecy, with the laying on of the hands of the presbytery.

Colossians 3 23 KJV And whatsoever ye do, do it heartedly, as to the Lord, and not unto men.

Romans 14 1 3 KJV Him that is weak in the faith receive ye, but not to doubtful disputations. 2 For one believeth that he may eat all things, another, who is weak, eateth herbs. 3 Let not him that eateth not, and let not him, which eateth not judge him that eateth, for God hath received him.

Romans 12 16 KJV Be of the same mind one toward another. Mind not high things, but condescend to men of low estate. Be not wise in your own conceits.

Hebrews 12 14 KJV Follow peace with all men, and holiness, without which no man shall see the Lord.

Proverbs 22 2 KJV The rich and poor meet together, the Lord is the maker of them all.

Romans 12 18 KJV If it be possible, as much as lieth in you, live peaceably with all men.

Colossians 3 25 KJV But he that doeth wrong shall receive for the wrong which he hath done; and there is no respect of persons.

Ecclesiastes 4 9 10 KJV Two are better than one, because they have a good reward for their labour. 10 For if they fall, the one will lift up his fellow; but woe to him that is alone when he falleth; for he hath not another to help him up.

Hebrews 3 13 KJV But exhort one another daily, while it is called Today, lest any of you be hardened through the deceitfulness of sin.

1 Peter 5 5 KJV Likewise, ye younger, submit yourselves unto the elder yea, all of you be subject one to another, and be clothed with humility, for God resisteth the proud, and giveth grace to the humble.

1 Peter 3 8 KJV Finally be ye all of one mind, having compassion one of another, love as brethren, be pitiful, be courteous.

1 John 1 7 KJV But if we walk in the light, as he is the light, we have fellowship one with another, and the blood of Jesus Christ his Son cleanseth us from all sin.

Isaiah 25 1 KJV O Lord, thou art my God; I will exalt thee, I will praise thy name; for thou hast done wonderful things; Thy counsels of old are faithfulness and truth.

Exodus 23 25 KJV And ye shall serve the Lord your God, and he shall bless thy bread, and thy water; and I will take sickness away from the midst of thee.

Psalm 150 6 KJV Let everything that have breath praise the Lord.

Matthew 25 30 KJV For I was an hungred, and ye gave me meat; I was thirsty, and ye gave me drink; I was a stranger, and ye took me in.

Galatians 6 2 KJV Bear ye one another's burdens, and so fulfil the law of Christ.

John 15 12 KJV This is my commandment, that ye love one another, as I have loved you.

Romans 15 1 KJV We then that are strong ought to bear the infirmities of the weak, and not to please ourselves.

John 13 34 KJV A new commandment I give unto you, That ye love one another as I have loved you, that ye also love one another.

1 John 4 7 KJV Beloved, let us love one another; for love is of God; and every one that loveth is born of God, and knoweth God.

Romans 12 10 KJV Be kindly affectioned one to another with brotherly love; in honour preferring one another.

1 John 4 11 KJV Beloved, if God so loved us, we ought also to love one another.

John 6 38 KJV For I came down from heaven, not to do mine own will, but the will of him that sent me.

Matthew 6 10 KJV Thy Kingdom come. Thy will be done in earth, as it is in heaven.

Ephesians 5 17 KJV Wherefore be ye not unwise, but understanding what the will of the Lord is.

Romans 8 28 KJV And we know that all things work together for good to them that love God, to them who are the called according to his purpose.

1 Corinthians 3 9 KJV For we are labourers together with God; ye are God's husbandry, ye are God's building.

Psalm 63 3 4 KJV Because thy loving kindness is better than life, my lips shall praise thee, Thus will I bless thee while I live; I will lift up my hands in thy name.

Colossians 3 16 KJV Let the word of Christ dwell in you richly in all wisdom, teaching and admonishing one another in psalms and hymns and spiritual songs.

1 Corinthians 15 58 KJV Be steadfast, immovable, always abounding in the work of the Lord.

Ephesians 6 11 KJV Put on the full armor of God, so that you will be able to stand firm against the schemes of the devil.

Mark 9 41 KJV For whosoever shall give you a cup of water to drink in my name, because ye belong to Christ, verily I say unto you, he shall not lose his reward.

Philippians 1 27 KJV Conduct yourselves in a manner worthy of the gospel of Christ, so that whether I come and see you or remain absent, I will hear of you that you are standing firm in one spirit, with one mind striving together for the faith of the gospel. Singing with grace in your hearts to the Lord.

Philippians 41 KJV Therefore, my beloved brethren whom I long to see, my joy and crown, in this way stand firm in the Lord, my beloved.

CHAPTER 23

Divorce, is a topic not really discussed, whereas an individual has any knowledge of it. God so joined together two people in hands together, united in marriage. A unity. When you first said, I do, you never dreamed that you would be saying someday, goodbye. God does not tear apart your marriage. It is the attacks of Satan that destroy, divide and cause many divisions. He came to rob, steal and destroy. There are many things going on, that can divert the attacks, and first and foremost, rely, and lean on God.

There are churches that help, and ministers should be available to you both. There are Christian marriage retreats, there is and are counselors and they put forth the effort to resolve the conflicts and try. With God, all things are possible. Should there be no other alternative than divorce and it is possible the person you married deserted you and abandoned you, then divorce is inevitable. It is hard enough to go around with your heart broken and not even know why. Or to even remotely understand however, you are now in this. You are not alone, as the heavenly father will never desert you or leave you. God will carry you. In the short of it, it is best to try and resolve things but when you can't and the other person flatly refuses, the best decision is to hire a good attorney to represent you. Most will even take payments in case you cannot afford one. To govern your well-being, you should not have war with the individual. If you have children that are involved, think and do what is best for them. Putting your personal feelings of attack aside. Go to your father and pray. By prayer and supplication, let your requests be known. Make sure you have everything you want to resolve and settle all down before you enter the court. To make someone suffer and drag things out in court for years is traumatic and undue suffering. Best to make the cut swiftly and move forward. I was drug through it, by mine, for 17 years and I can personally tell you it is devasting and nothing is worth losing one moment of your life over for that or anything. You can do without and you most certainly can take your time to adjust and work and do what is needed. To make a life for you and if children the best. One person cannot make that much difference, that you have to go through anything that will ruin the best that God has for you. No one said, it would or will be easy, but with your father and in this, you are not alone and you will triumph. It may seem like you are alone, but you are not. Surround yourself with friends and family, and join a church and fellowship. Most of all, do not go to friends and ask to seek opinions. The only true answer is God, and you have the time to wait upon him. You can do this.

Afterward decide if you want another relationship and leave your heart open for him to guide you. Do not jump at the first chance to rebound with another relationship. It seldom works and sometimes you just want to be happy and alone. Whatever it is, give yourself some time and let God direct your path. Do something for others, be of service, and don't mope around as that will leave you empty and, more often than not, into depression or a pity party. Thank God for the time and the happiness with this person, forgive, and move forward. God loves you and he will never leave you and will always be there for you in everything.

2 Corinthians 5 7 KJV For we walk by faith not sight.

Hebrews 11 6 KJV But without faith it is impossible to please him; for he hath cometh to God must believe that he is, and that he is a rewarder of them that diligently seek him.

Romans 10 17 KJV So then faith cometh by hearing and hearing by the word of God.

Hebrews 11 1 KJV Now faith is the substance of things hoped for, the evidence of things not seen.

Psalms 63 1 KJV (A Psalm of David, when he was in the wilderness of Judah.) O God; early will I seek thee, my soul thirsteth for thee, my flesh longeth for thee in a dry and thirsty land, where no water is.

John 17 22 KJV And the glory which thou gavest me I have given them; that they may be one, even as we are one.

Jeremiah 29 11 KJV For I know the thoughts that I think toward you saith the Lord, thoughts of peace and not of evil, to give you and expected end.

John 14 18 KJV I will not leave you comfortless; I will come to you.

John 14 26 KJV But the Comforter, which is the Holy Ghost, whom the Father will send in my name he shall teach you all things, and bring all things, to your remembrance, whatsoever I have said unto you.

Matthew 5 4 KJV Blessed are they that mourn; for they shall be comforted.

John 15 26 KJV But when the Comforter is come, whom I will send unto you from the Father, even the Spirit of truth, which proceedeth from the Father, he shall testify of me.

Jeremiah 17 14 KJV Heal me, Oh Lord, and I shall be healed; save me, and I shall be saved; for thou art my praise.

Jeremiah 33 6 KJV Behold, I will bring it health and cure, and I will cure them, and will reveal unto them the abundance of peace and truth.

Psalm 147 3 KJV He healeth the broken in heart, and bindeth up their wounds.

3 John 2 KJV 1 2 KJV Beloved, I wish above all things that thou mayest prosper and be in health, even as thy soul prosperous.

Ephesians 6 11 KJV Put on the whole armour of God, that ye may be able to stand against the wiles of the devil.

Psalm 32 7 KJV Thou art my hiding place; thou shalt preserve me from trouble; thou shalt compas me about with songs of deliverance.

Hebrews 11 1 KJV Now the faith is the substance of things hoped for, the evidence of things not seen.

Romans 5 1 KJV Therefore being justified by faith, we have peace with God through our Lord Jesus Christ.

Exodus 15 2 KJV The Lord is my strength and song, and he is become my salvation; he is my God's and I will prepare him an habitation; my father God, and I will exalt him.

Isaiah 41 10 KJV Fear thou not; for I am with thee; be not dismayed, for I am thy God; I will strengthen thee, yea, I will help thee, yea, I will uphold thee with the right hand of my righteousness.

Matthew 28 20 KJV Teaching them to observe all things what so ever I have commanded you; and, lo, I am with you always, even unto the end of the world.

Isaiah 41 13 KJV For I the Lord thy God will hold thy right hand, saying unto thee, Fear not, I will keep thee.

Psalm 73 26 KJV My flesh and my heart faileth; but God is the strength of my heart, and my portion for ever.

Psalm 121 1 2 KJV I will lift up mine eyes unto the hills, from whence cometh my help. My help cometh from the Lord, which made heaven and earth.

Isaiah 40 29 KJV He giveth power to the faint; and to them that have no might he increaseth strength.

Exodus 14 14 KJV The Lord shall fight for you, and ye shall hold your peace.

Isaiah 558 KJV For my thoughts are not your thoughts, neither your ways my ways, saith the Lord.

Psalm 128 1 KJV Blessed is everyone that feareth the Lord; that walketh in his ways.

Proverbs 3 31 32 KJV Envy thou not the oppressors, and choose none of his ways. For the froward is abomination to the Lord; but his secret is with the righteous.

Hebrews 13 5 KJV Let your conversation be without covetousness and be content with such things as ye have; for he hath said, I will never leave thee, nor forsake thee.

ISAIAH 41 10 KJV Fear thou not, for I am with thee, be not dismayed; for I am thy God; I will strengthen thee; yea. I will help thee, yea, I will uphold thee with the right hand of my righteousness.

Hebrews 13 6 KJV So that we may boldly say, The Lord is my helper, and I will not fear what man shall do unto me.

Timothy 11 7 KJV For God hath not given us the spirit of fear; but of power, and of love, and of a sound mind.

Romans 12 12 KJV Rejoicing in hope; patient in tribulation, continuing instant in prayer.

Exodus 14 14 KJV The Lord shall fight for you, and you shall hold your peace.

Luke 1 37 KJV For with God nothing shall be impossible.

Mark 11 24 KJV Therefore I say unto you, what things soever ye desire, when ye pray, believe that ye receive them, and ye shall have them.

Jeremiah 32 27 KJV Behold, I am the Lord, the God of all flesh; is there any thing to hard for me?

CHAPTER 24

In lack, yes, lack, know God is. He will provide. He loads us daily with benefits. If you are facing a hardship, don't despair. Things are provided that you need. There is a difference of wants and desires. Those our father gives too. He meets those needs. By Jesus blood, we claim his righteous, not lacking. Forgiven our sins, health, not sickness. God is the answer. God is all. Do not give into the flesh our self-lusts, greed, and temptations. Stand on God's promises. He is a firm, solid foundation. Waiting on him patiently. You will see him move in many ways. Give thanks and Glory to his name always. This event, yes, the event may last a moment or a season; but God's love lasts forever. Things will get better, and my friend, so will you! Each day you can repeat some positive phrases that uplift and encourage you.

Such as, I am getting better and better every day in every way, He is the way, the source. I will because God says I can. God wants me to live abundantly. Fill yourself daily with God's word and set time for you and our heavenly Father to sit and talk, to even laugh and yes, to cry. He knows and he sees. He does not want his children, or his family, to suffer. We must stand strong in our relationship with Father, Son and Holy Spirit. Enough comes each day, and we must rely on Him always. Not in large things, but in ALL things! Large and small. Stuff comes and goes, but family, and love is forever. Open up your heart to God and let the sun shine in, as he, God, is radiant. You will shine. Yesterday you can't get back, tomorrow is not here. Yet today and every day is a special gift. He is that gift today. Thank him. Be a blessing to someone. A smile, a hug, a cup of coffee. Whatever, you will see God's love coming to you. He is awesome and so, so amazing.

Bills will always be there, taxes, debts, you have gotten there, make a way little by little to totally, depend on God. Starting over, loss, we can because God says we can. Let God in today. Right now. Ask God to enter your life, and accept Jesus as your personal savior. The victory belongs to you, the battle belongs to God. Jesus bore our sins on the cross and gave his life for you and me. Our sins. May you find love and joy on your journey. Jesus has the victory and is victorious. He can do all things. Let him walk with you in all things. He fills my life with good things.

Psalm 103 5 NLT See for yourself the mercies shown down on all who trust in him. If you belong to the Lord, reverence him; for everyone who does this has everything he needs.

Peter 3 7 KJV Likewise, ye husbands, dwell with them accordingly to knowledge, giving honour unto the wife, as unto the weaker vessel, and as being heirs together of the grace of life; that your prayers be not hindered.

Ephesians 5 25 KJV Husbands, love your wives, even as Christ also loved the church, and gave himself for it.

Ephesians 6 12 KJV For we wrestle not against flesh and blood, but against principalities, against powers, against the rulers of the darkness of this world, against spiritual wickedness in high places.

Romans 12 19 KJV Dearly beloved, avenge not yourselves, but rather give place unto wrath, for it is written, vengeance is mine, I will repay saith the Lord.

Luke 10 19 KJV Behold, I give unto you power to tread on serpents and scorpions, and over all the power of the enemy; and nothing shall by any means hurt you.

Romans 12 21 KJV Be not overcome of evil, but overcome evil with good.

James 4 7 KJV Submit yourselves therefore to God. Resist the devil, and he will flee from you.

John 14 15 KJV If ye love me, keep my commandments.

Hebrews 4 12 KJV For the word of God is quick, and powerful, and sharper than any two-edged sword, piercing even to the dividing asunder of soul and spirit, and of the joints and marrow, and is a discerner of the thoughts and intents of the heart.

Isaiah 41 13 KJV For I thee Lord thy God will hold thy right hand, saying unto thee, Fear not; I will help thee.

Psalms 18 2 KJV The Lord is my rock, and my fortress, and my deliverer; my God, my strength, in whom I will trust; my buckler, and the horn of my salvation, and my high tower.

12 2 KJV And be not conformed to this world, but be ye transformed by the renewing of your mind, that ye may prove what is good, and acceptable, and perfect, will of God.

Romans 8 37 KJV Nay, in all these things we are more than conquerors through him that loved us.

Hebrews 13 5 KJV Let your conversation be without covetousness; and be content with such things as ye have; for he hath said; I will never leave thee, nor forsake thee.

Matthew 28 20 KJV Teaching them to observe all things whatsoever I have commanded you, and, lo, I am with you always, even unto the end of the world. Amen.

Psalm 145 18 KJV The Lord is nigh unto all them that call upon him, to all that call upon him in truth. He will fulfill the desire of them that fear him; he also will hear their cry, and will save them.

Psalm 37 4 KJV Delight thyself also in the Lord; and he shall give thee the desires of thine heart.

Isaiah 46 4 KJV And even to your old age I am he; and even to hoar hairs will I carry you; I have made, and I will bear; even I carry, and deliver you.

1 John 4 4 KJV Ye are of God, little children, and have overcome them because greater is he that is he that is in you, than he that is in the world.

Job 33 12 KJV Behold, in this thou art not just; I will answer thee, that God is greater than man.

1 Peter 4 10 KJV As every man hath received the gift, even so minister the same one to another, as good stewards of the manifold grace of God.

Luke 6 38 KJV Give, and it shall be given unto you; good measure, pressed down, and shaken together, and running over, shall men give into your bosom. For with the same measure that ye mete withal it shall be measured to you again.

Matthew 5 16 KJV Let your light so shine before men, that they may see your good works, and glorify your Father which is in heaven.

CONCLUSION

My hope for you is that you can open your hearts to God and see how amazing He is. With the Father and Son, you can do anything. In life, there are many trials and things that you will go through and if I can lessen the pain and assist you in avoiding the hurt, and resting in God, then that is what my desire is, to see you happy and not having to suffer at the hands of a situation, you are uncertain about and may fester and be carried along for years because someone or something hurt you. You can enjoy your life and open your heart and surrender to our Father and live the life you are designed to live. For years, I have carried the hurt of many people, and by no means mine to carry. I wish that I had opened my heart sooner and known a different way in which to embark and know I have and had my father to lean on. Especially in loving someone who I shared many years with and to this day will always love them with all my heart, no matter how much pain and suffering they inflicted upon me, because they themselves were hurting. Abandonment. Wanting my will and way before resting in the fathers. Complete surrender, and love for our Father and being totally obedient to him. It does not mean that we are perfect, nor does it mean we can earn merits or a place in heaven, but knowing that God gave his son to die for our sins and that by his blood shed, we are saved, and forgiven our sins, is the greatest gift anyone could ever give you or I. Welcome him into your life now and watch the amazing transformation you will experience as you walk and grow in Christ. Allow him to be the director and navigator and your compass. He loves you very much, and today you can make that change. Dare to take his hand to the promised land. There is nothing, absolutely nothing in this world, that has a right to hurt you, take one moment of joy from you, rob you of the gifts that God has given you, or anyone that has a right to hurt another and lose from that blow, hurt, or loss. Take it as a memory and place it into your heart. Take that loss and count it as a gain. Take that pain and turn it into something positive and return the pain with joy and thanksgiving. He is truly amazing. I wish you love and happiness. You decide if you want to carry it forever or if you want the course the heavenly father has set for you, and take his hand to the promised land. God bless you always.

www.ingramcontent.com/pod-product-compliance
Lightning Source LLC
Chambersburg PA
CBHW072332150726
47998CB00017B/502